C000000141

TOWNS & VILLAGES OF BRITAIN: WEST YORKSHIRE

John Spencer

Series editor: Terry Marsh

Copyright © J. Spencer, 2000

All Rights Reserved. No part of this publication may be reproduced, stored in a retrieval system, or transmitted in any form or by any means – electronic, mechanical, photocopying, recording, or otherwise – without prior written permission from the publisher or a licence permitting restricted copying issued by the Copyright Licensing Agency, 90 Tottenham Court Road, London W1P 0LA. This book may not be lent, resold, hired out or otherwise disposed of by trade in any form of binding or cover other than that in which it is published, without the prior consent of the publisher.

Published by Sigma Leisure – an imprint of
Sigma Press, 1 South Oak Lane, Wilmslow, Cheshire SK9 6AR, England.

British Library Cataloguing in Publication Data
A CIP record for this book is available from the British Library.

ISBN: 1-85058-647-0

Series Editor: Terry Marsh

Typesetting and Design by: Sigma Press, Wilmslow, Cheshire.

Cover Design: MFP Design & Print

Cover photographs: main photograph – Holmfirth; smaller pictures – from top: Morrland farm scene; mill valley, Colne Valley; Tunnel End, Colne Valley

Photographs: by the author, except where otherwise acknowledged

Map: Morag Perrott

Printed by: MFP Design & Print

Contents

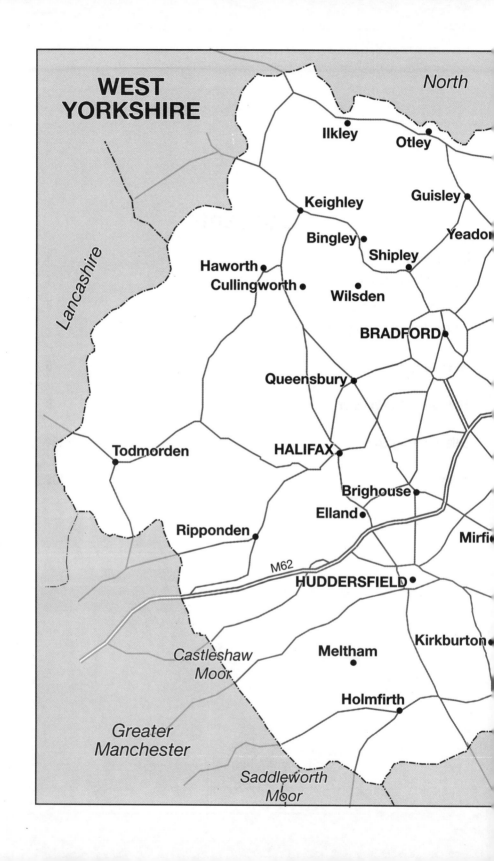

Introduction

The 'Towns and Villages of Britain' is a series of titles detailing a county-by-county approach to the many delights and fascinations of our country's cities, towns, villages and hamlets. There is much of interest and value throughout our towns and villages, but not all of it is widely documented, and some of it, particularly local customs, folklore and traditions, is in danger of being lost forever. By bringing all this information together, county-by-county, it becomes possible to build a unique and substantially comprehensive library of knowledge.

All of the books in the series are compiled to the same specification and in gazetteer format, and include information about the way or the reason a town or village evolved; references to anything associated with the preservation of the past, such as museums, heritage centres, historic or prehistoric sites, battle sites, places of worship and other locally or architecturally important buildings. Landscape features are also detailed, including important natural history sites, geological sites, water features, etc. as is information about important local people, and details of events. There are also notes about any significant present-day informal amenity/recreational features, like country parks, open access land, Areas of Outstanding Natural Beauty, nature reserves, and Sites of Special Scientific Interest. Finally, information is given on any significant Roman or prehistory context, and any anecdotal or endemic folklore references associated with the town or village which might illustrate a particular way of life or social development. The books are therefore eminently suitable for anyone interested in their own locality or in local history; students of history, folklore and related subjects; professional journalists wanting up-to-date and comprehensive information; public relations and similar businesses; photographers and artists, and, of course, the tourists and visitors to the counties.

Explanatory Notes

It has been suggested that to qualify as a village, a 'community' must possess a school, a pub, a post office and a church. Such a requirement, however, excludes a large number of places that are of immense interest, many having important historical associations, and which have played a vital part in the development of the county and its people. So, for the purposes of the books in this series, the criteria for inclusion have been kept deliberately simple: there must be something of interest about the place; or it must have associations with events and people of countywide or wider significance.

Often, the 'something of interest' will simply be the village church (its history, contents or architecture), or its green or a river bridge. In addition, the village may be important to the heritage of the county because it maintains the traditions, ways and beliefs of local culture, or has played a key role in the social, economic or political history of the county or the country as a whole.

Only occasionally, however, is the village pub of special interest in this context, and often the development of large supermarkets within easy travelling distance of the villages has, sadly, signalled the demise of the traditional village shop. Local schools have often been swallowed up by larger schools, and far too many post offices are proving difficult to sustain as viable concerns. So, while that 'classic' definition of a village has much to commend it, in reality it is today too restrictive.

Quite what makes a town is another, arguable, matter. But the precise definition is not too important here; it's the place and its people, not its status, that matters. As a very broad distinction, that no-one should take seriously, a 'hamlet' (a few of which appear in these books) is a distinct community, while a 'village' could be said to be a hamlet with a church, and a 'town' is a village with a market.

In many cases, the historical development of the community, whether a tiny village, a town or a city, is fascinating in itself, and so it is that each entry gradually builds up a picture of the county

that is unique. That is what this book endeavours to portray, in a logical and easily accessible way, as well as being a source of reference.

Inevitably, there will be places that have been omitted that others might argue should have been included. But the value each community has to bring to a work of this nature has been carefully weighed; invariably, borderline cases have been given the benefit of the doubt and included.

It is equally clear that, taken to its logical conclusion, this book would be ten times larger, and there has had to be a considerable degree of selective editing to make it of manageable size. One day, perhaps, there could be one book that says everything there is to say about the county, but could we afford to buy it? Could we carry it? Would we want it, when part of the beauty of what does exist is the range of voices and shades of opinion so many different authors can bring?

Following the General Introduction, the book becomes a gazetteer, listing the towns and villages of the county in alphabetical order.

① After each town or village name there appears, in square brackets, [ ], the name of the relevant district council (see below).

① Next appears a two-letter, four-figure grid reference, which will pinpoint the settlement to within half a mile (one kilometre). This is followed by an approximate distance from some other, usually larger, settlement, together with an equally approximate direction indicator.

ⓘ Those features or people 'of interest' directly associated with the settlement are highlighted in bold text, while an index lists other features or people only incidentally associated.

ⓘ Where information is given about events, such as agricultural shows, or facilities, such as museums, details of dates and hours of opening are usually available from any of the Tourist Information Centres listed below.

Information Centres

Bradford: Central Library, Princes Way, Bradford, BD1 1NN. Tel: 01274 753678; Fax: 01274 739067; Open: Jan-Dec.

Halifax: Piece Hall, Halifax, HX1 1RE. Tel: 01422 368725; Fax: 01422 354264; Open: Jan-Dec.

Haworth: 2-4 West Lane, Haworth, BD22 8EF. Tel: 01535 642329; Fax: 01535 647721; Open: Jan-Dec.

Hebden Bridge: 1 Bridge Gate, Hebden Bridge, HX7 8EX. Tel: 01422 843831; Fax: 01422 845266; Open: Jan-Dec.

Holmfirth: 49-51 Huddersfield Road, Holmfirth, HD7 1JP. Tel: 01484 222444; Fax: 01484 222445.

Huddersfield: 3-5 Albion Street, Huddersfield, HD1 2NW. Tel: 01484 223200; Fax: 01484 223202; Open: Jan-Dec.

Ilkley: Station Road, Ilkley, LS29 8HA. Tel: 01943 602319; Fax: 01943 603795; Open: Jan-Dec.

Leeds: Gateway Yorkshire, PO Box 244, The Arcade, City Station, Leeds, LS1 1PL. Tel: 0113 2425242; Fax: 0113 2468246; Open: Jan-Dec.

Saltaire: 2 Victoria Road, Shipley, BD18 3LA. Tel: 01274 774993; Fax: 01274 774464; Open Jan-Dec.

Todmorden: 15 Burnley Road, Todmorden, OL14 7BU. Tel: 01706 818181; Open: Jan-Dec.

Wakefield: Town Hall, Wood Street, Wakefield, WF1 2HQ. Tel: 01924 305000; Fax: 01924 305775; Open: Jan-Dec.

Wetherby: Council Offices, 24 Westgate, Wetherby, LS22 6NL. Tel: 0113 2477251; Fax: 0113 2477251; Open: Jan-Dec.

West Yorkshire on the Internet

There are several World Wide Web sites relevant both to tourists and residents of the area. Currently (autumn 1999) there are some useful and well-designed local government sites that are useful jumping-off points, such as:

www.leeds.gov.uk

www. wakefield.gov.uk

www.calderdale.gov.uk

Equally interesting are those that

serve local communities,
including:

www.kirklees.com

www.eclipse.co.uk/pens/

www.kbf.co.uk/bronte.htm
- the Kirklees site is obvious
enough, but the second one is an
interesting and unusual one, being
all about the creative folk of Hebden Bridge (writers, artists and the
like), while the last one is an excellent source of information for
Brontë enthusiasts.

This really is the tip of the internet
iceberg - be warned that a search
for "West Yorkshire" will produce
thousands of "hits".

West Yorkshire

If those who reorganised the local government of England and Wales in 1974 have anything at all to be thanked for – and until now the author could think of nothing – it was for reducing the size of what we now know as 'West Yorkshire'. The view is an entirely personal one, based on the realisation that the already daunting task of compiling a book on its towns and villages would have been even more so a quarter of a century ago.

Then, the West Riding was the largest of three 'thridings' or thirds, created as administrative districts by the Vikings when they came to settle these parts in the 9th century. It stretched from Sheffield 'in the county of Hallamshire' in the south to Sedbergh and the Howgill Fells in the far north-west; and from Swinefleet, on the border with Lincolnshire, in the east to Bentham and Slaidburn in the west. It included the great city of York, home to the Danish Vikings, and Harrogate, Settle and Malham, Doncaster and Rotherham and Barnsley.

After 1974, the Ridings disappeared, to be replaced by what many considered to be aberrations. North Yorkshire is easy enough to understand – being most of the North Riding and a bit of the West. The county of West Yorkshire was likewise logical, in that it contained the main industrial cities of the former West Riding: Bradford, Leeds, Huddersfield and Halifax. But what, and where, was Humberside? Hull and its surrounding lands had been the East Riding for a thousand years – a bureaucrat's pen was unlikely to end that, as further reorganisation since has proved. As for South Yorkshire – dubbed 'the Socialist Republic' by one of the county's few Conservative councillors at the height of the Thatcher years – that, too, was an incongruity, but one which has yet to be rectified.

All that said, it means that this volume follows the boundary of the former Metropolitan County of West Yorkshire, an area still made up by the local authorities of Wakefield and Kirklees in the south, of Calderdale and Bradford to the west, and Leeds in the north-east. It is a logical area as far as the history of the last century and a half is concerned, much of it having been reshaped by the benefits, and destruction, brought by the Industrial Revolution and its aftermath. Unfortunately for the historian interested in a broader span of time, the coming of the factories, the mills, the engineering works and the great towns and cities often meant the disappearance of much fine architecture and interesting landscapes, which survived elsewhere. Nonetheless, fine Norman, even Anglo-Saxon, churches do survive, as do even more medieval structures together with one or two villages which seem to have been preserved in a time warp, oblivious of the tumult around them. In a way, the changes should be seen as a virtue; the unexpected ancient gems are always more greatly appreciated than the commonplace.

And while West Yorkshire might not be groaning with cruck barns and mullioned old manor houses, it does have some of the most important Victorian and Edwardian architecture in the country. Indeed, in some places, such as Bradford or Halifax, whole townscapes seem to have been preserved for the visitor to explore and enjoy.

And make no mistake, these towns, like their neighbours over the Pennines in Lancashire, were the manufacturing powerhouses that helped make Victorian Britain's power and influence in the world. Yorkshire woollens and worsteds, made in mills powered by Yorkshire coal, on machines built in Yorkshire engineering works, spanned the globe for a century or more. And while the 19th century was the apogee of the textile industry, it was an industry that had been associated with the area since ancient times. It didn't take a particularly intelligent Anglo-Saxon or Viking farmer to realise that large tracts of the West Yorkshire landscape were unsuited to the forms of arable farming undertaken in the Vale of York, or the flatlands of Lincolnshire and Nottinghamshire. On the Pennine hills it rained half the year, and snowed when it wasn't raining. The only things likely to survive here were hardy oats and barley, sheep, and the tough breed of human beings that ate all three.

Brontë Parsonage Museum

The sheep, though, were a valuable asset, and only consigned to the pot when their days of providing milk and wool were over. By the early Middle Ages, Cistercian monks were farming tens of thousands of sheep on West Yorkshire's moors and fostering a trade which by the end of the 14th century made England one of the richest kingdoms in Western Europe. Yorkshire wool from the bleak, peaty uplands would be exported to the Low Countries – it formed the basis of the wealth of cities such as Ghent and Bruges in Flanders – worked there, and then reimported as cloth for garments.

By Elizabethan times, the woollen trade was thriving in West Yorkshire, with towns such as Leeds, Halifax and Wakefield all having substantial and important cloth halls where local weavers would bring their home-made 'pieces' for sale to merchant clothiers. The tough conditions of such an existence meant that most homes clinging to the valleys of the Aire, Calder and Colne would grow some basic crops, such as a few vegetables, and possess a small flock of sheep. The stone-built family home would have a long room spanning the length of the building where the man of the house would weave the yarn spun downstairs on a tradi-tional spinning wheel by his wife and daughters. The top storey would have mullioned windows across its whole length, and wher-ever possible these 'weaver's cot-tages' would face south to make the most of the available daylight. In good years, it was enough to keep the wolf from the door.

Bustling Haworth – home of West Yorkshire's most important literary family,

To the east, away from the moors, a different, but equally hard living was eked. Here, the climate might not be as bleak, but the land was often flooded by the wide rivers which ran through it and many folk found themselves in the hard and dangerous pursuits of coal and ironstone mining.

The end of the 18th century brought huge advances in technology, and turned the small villages and towns of West Yorkshire into noisy, unhealthy but vital cauldrons of industry. The end of the 'domestic system' of textile manufacture affected both woollen and cotton spinners and weavers – and both products were made on this side of the Pennines until well into the 1850s. These giant machines needed huge buildings to house them, and huge workforces to tame them – they also had huge appetites and transformed the lives of those who lived above the rich reserves of the Yorkshire coalfield.

While cities grew, new roads replaced those that, although built by the Romans, had long stood the test of time linking age-old commercial centres. Now, supplies had to reach towns that decades earlier had been mere hamlets, and their produce had to be transported away to market. West Yorkshire's turnpike roads provided an early solution but were soon superseded by the canals, before the coming of the railways overtook both.

By the end of the Victorian era, the former townships of Leeds, Bradford and Huddersfield were clothing the world – and their buildings, parks and churches reflected that fact. Things have changed in the century since; recession, depression and the inevitable flood of cheap imports from abroad have all taken their toll. But much remains of what made West Yorkshire great, both in bricks and mortar, and in the spirit of its people. The cities of Leeds and Bradford remain major commercial and manufacturing centres – the products might have changed, but the virtues that go into them have not. Better yet for the visitor, much of the county's history has been preserved in some excellent museums and related attractions. This book can never claim to list them all. Instead, it provides a detailed cross-section of what this fascinating county has to offer – and what a lot there is.

The Towns and Villages

ABERFORD [Leeds]

SE4337: 3 miles (5km) NE of Garforth

This attractive village is best reached via the A1, a highway responsible in part for Aberford's prosperity. The road – when known as 'the Great North Road' and the historic highway between London and York – once ran straight through the village, and the coaching inns that grew up as a result still exist.

Particularly interesting are the Gothic **almshouses**, which have been put to more modern use as craft and other shops. The **church of St Ricarius** is essentially a creation of the middle of the last century. A close look, however, reveals a Norman window (look for the curved arch) and there is also the fragment of an Anglo-Saxon cross.

Nearby is **Parlington Park**, a pleasant place to take a walk and the site of a magnificent **triumphal arch.** It has three archways and is the work of Thomas Leverton. The inscription 'Liberty in N. America triumphant' and the date 1783 refer to the American War of Independence.

ACKWORTH [Wakefield]

SE4417: 3 miles (5km) N of Hemsworth

Standing in the heart of what was once the thriving West Yorkshire coalfield, the community of Ackworth has suffered far less than many of its neighbouring towns and villages. Largely due to its close communications with Wakefield and Leeds, the village has a settled 'dormitory' feel and rural aspects all round. The **church of St Cuthbert** is pleasing to look at, but Victorian in design and largely dating from the 1850s.

Driving through the village, look out for the stone post dated 1805 directly opposite the **Friends' School** or 'Quaker School' as it is almost universally known. Dating back to the middle of the 18th century, the original building was a Foundling Hospital. Perhaps Ackworth had a shortage of orphans and otherwise deserted infants, because in 1779 it took on a new role as a Quaker School – one for which it has been famed ever since.

The industrial north was a happy recruiting ground for the many Nonconformist varieties of the Christian following which flourished in the 1700s, with the Society of Friends, or Quakers, having significant support in the West Riding. Founded by George Fox in the middle of the 17th century, it neglected to adopt either specific creed or regular ministry. The label 'Quakers' was reputedly coined by Justice Bennett of Derby who said Fox 'bid them tremble at the Word of the Lord'. Tremble or not, the school has an excellent record and reputation, particularly for the liberality of its teaching, and is very popular to this day.

Just north of the village, look out for the **plague stone** which was used as a place where food and medicines could be exchanged for money from helpful neighbours in times of pestilence.

ADDINGHAM [Calderdale]

SE0749: 5½ miles (9km) N of Keighley

Close to the River Wharfe, this pleasant village was once the home of more than half a dozen woollen mills and prior to that, in the 18th century, housed workers in the weaving workshops – one of which still exists. Soon these semi-independent tradespeople, working for a well-to-do yeoman merchant clothier, would find themselves having to toil in the larger mills that characterised much of the county in the Industrial Revolution.

The Victorian novelist Elizabeth ('Mrs') Gaskell mentions Addingham in her *Life of Charlotte Brontë*. The author of *Cranford*, *Mary Barton* and other books vividly charting the life and mores of industrial Britain relates an incident in which she and her husband, researching the Brontë biography, saw a boy jump into a stream and cut himself badly on discarded glass. Litter louts and their consequences are not an exclusively modern bane.

Addingham's history goes much further back, however, the village having grown up close to a Roman highway. In 970, Archbishop Wulfere of York is reputed to have fled to Addingham to evade the pillaging Danes who had attacked his own city. If he did, he will have sought refuge in the only substantial building the settlement will have had at that time, **the church of St Peter**. Standing on an attractive green and reached over the beck via a stone bridge, the church as now seen is mainly mid-18th century. However, it has Perpendicular features of three centuries earlier and an Anglo-Saxon cross is positive proof that a much earlier ecclesiastical building stood on the site. Who knows, the timorous Wulfere might well have knelt and worshipped at it.

A cutting of the fabled 'Glastonbury Thorn' is said to grow in the churchyard. Harking back to English Christianity's earliest times, the Thorn is said to have sprouted from the staff of Joseph of Arimathea, the man who brought what was then a new religion, together with the Holy Grail, to this island in AD63. Glastonbury, an ancient town in Somerset, has much pre-Christian history and is close to Cadbury Castle, the legendary site of Arthur's Camelot. Joseph's staff not only took root, but also budded and supposedly blossoms each old Christmas Day. The name 'Glastonbury Thorn' is now given to a variety of hawthorn, a common tree in many an ancient churchyard.

ADEL [Leeds]

SE2739: 4½ miles (7km) NW of Leeds

On the Otley road out of Leeds, this is both a traditional community and a popular home for commuters employed in the nearby city. An open aspect is maintained by Headingley Golf Club, which ensures the development of recent years does not stray across the whole of this pleasant rural area.

Most notable for the visitor is the **church of St John the Baptist,** a 12th-century Norman building of major national importance. One of the most complete Norman churches in the north of England, it has delights both inside and out – much of the carving retaining remarkable vitality and line after nearly 900 years. The south aisle door (dated as of around 1150) is truly remarkable, with the signature zigzag or 'dog's tooth' carving, together with carvings of Christ, the Lamb of God, and symbols of the Evangelists. Just stand back and see how much you can identify. The door itself has a fascinating Norman ring-handle showing a monster eating a man and is known as a 'sanctuary knocker'. Inside, the marvels continue in an aisle-less nave. There is more zigzag moulding in the chancel arch, and 37 carved heads – all of them different. Feast your eyes on a range of other designs, the work of stonemasons chipping away when York Minster was a small place of worship.

Not far from the church is Adel Mill, now an upmarket residential development, but dating back much further. The current mill is thought to date from the 1600s, with the barn of a century or so later. Experts believe a monastery may have once stood on the site, and that earlier still it was a Roman encampment.

ALLERTON BYWATER [Leeds]

SE4227: 2 miles (3km) NW of Castleford

This small settlement is more interesting for its location and place in the development of the Industrial Revolution than any specific building. Nonetheless, situated close to the junction of the Rivers Aire and Calder, it has seen much activity. The 150 years following the latter half of the 18th century must have been particularly bustling as the Aire and Calder Navigation allowed vast quantities of water-borne traffic to pass the village.

While during much of the 1700s and onwards, wily investors were pumping money into the cutting of canals, like-minded money-men were adapting rivers as navigable watercourses. Meanders were straightened, banks reinforced, channels dredged and, where necessary, locks installed. The company responsible for the Aire and Calder Navigation owned a range of other waterways and, amongst other things, founded the port of Goole in the 1820s.

ALMONDBURY [Kirklees]

SE1615: 2 miles (3km) SE of Huddersfield

Sitting comfortably on a hillside above the much bigger neighbouring town of Huddersfield, it is easy to see why many prosperous Victorian businessmen and mill owners chose to desert the smog and perch themselves here. Many of their grand homes still survive, together with the once-cobbled streets lined with the terraced homes of the ordinary, hard-working folk they employed.

Almondbury's history is an ancient one and it appears in the Domesday Book of 1086 as 'Alemanberie'. Prior to the Industrial Revolution, wool markets were held here and the important **parish church of All Hallows** bears testament to the longstanding prosperity of the local community. Dating from the later 15th century and in the Perpendicular style, but with some Early English features (13th century), it contains some important medieval stained glass. Some of this is the work of some of the country's greatest glass craftsmen who also worked on York Minster. The nave roof is stunning in its detail, and of particular importance to those keen on such things is the font cover. It dates back to the 1500s and is considered to be the finest example in the region.

Other interesting sites in the village include, in Westgate, the half-timbered **Wormall Hall**. The hall is dated 1631 and has the initials 'IWM' carved on the lintel. Although now the local Conservative Club, the hall was the home of wealthy Isaac Wormhall and a carriage archway can be seen on the left of the stone-built ground floor.

King James's Grammar School, also thought to date back to the early 17th century, is an interesting example of an early English educational institution, while Almondbury still has its own 'common', an enclosed piece of land where locals used to gather for various fun-filled holiday activities. Historians record that one such recreation, bull baiting, had its final performance on Rush-Bearing Day (the first Monday in August) 1824. While bull baiting needs little explanation, rush-bearing celebrated the renewal of the rushes with which the church floor would be strewn in medieval times. The rushes protected the ill-shod feet of worshippers from the chilling flagstones in winter. Some churches document fees for hedgehogs that were released into the building at the same time as new rushes were laid. The hedgehogs were to keep down the insects that inevitably came with the rushes.

Another attraction for visitors to this interesting part of Kirklees is **Castle Hill**. Easy to find, even if the signposts weren't available, the tower on the top of the hill is visible for miles around and serves as an easy guidepost. The **Jubilee Tower** itself was built in 1899 to commemorate Queen Victoria's Diamond Jubilee. It is easy to see why the site was chosen, man has been celebrating and occupying this prominent site for at least 4000 years.

Archaeologists reckon the hill, which dominates the Colne and

Holme Valleys from a height of 900ft (300m), and has steep climbs on three sides, was occupied by Neolithic man. They built a simple earthen bank and ditch structure; while 1500 years later Iron Age Settlers built a fortress here. In the 12th century, during King Stephen's reign, the Normans rebuilt the long neglected banks, dug a huge ditch and built a stone keep. The castle was dismantled by Henry III.

A pub was first built on Castle Hill during the Napoleonic Wars, with the current building dating back to the 1850s. Beacons were traditionally sited on the hill – on a clear day the whole of the Vale of York is visible from here – a tradition revived in recent years for significant national events.

ALTOFTS [Wakefield]

SE3723: 3 miles (5km) NE of Wakefield

Set in the heart of the Yorkshire coalfield, this town has prospered, and suffered, with the coal industry's rise and ultimate sad decline. Now a commuter-base for more prosperous towns and cities, Altofts was an agricultural settlement once dominated by the long-since demolished **Frobisher Hall**. Arguably the town's most famous son, Sir Martin Frobisher was resident there once. He had been sent to sea as a boy in the 1540s and set sail in 1576 in search of a north-west passage to 'Cathay'. Disaster struck off Greenland, but Frobisher made Labrador, where a bay still bears his name. In 1585 he sailed with Drake to the West Indies and three years later was knighted by Elizabeth I for his actions as commander of the *Triumph* against the Spanish Armada. He was mortally wounded at the siege of Crozon, near Brest in France in 1594.

During the last century the need for coal led to the discovery of healthy seams in the area, including the Silkstone, named after the South Yorkshire village some miles away where it outcropped. Mining at Altofts provided much employment – so much so that the colliery owners built their own settlement, known as 'the Buildings', to house their workers. With predictable class distinction, there were different standards of properties for foremen – or deputies – officials and miners. In addition, and in keeping with similar ventures elsewhere, the colliery company also built a school, a co-operative store and -of course - a Wesleyan Chapel to ensure nobody stepped out of line on Sundays.

Much mould-breaking mines' rescue and safety work was done at Altofts, but the decline in the industry meant this proud tradition is now little more than a memory. The vast majority of the 'Buildings' have now been demolished.

Worth a look around if you are in the vicinity is the **parish church of St Mary Magdelene,** which dates back to the 1880s. The reredos – the structure behind the altar – has an attractive Italianate mosaic and the stained-glass windows are by the acclaimed Victorian artist C.E. Kempe.

ALVERTHORPE [Wakefield]

SE3021: 2 miles (3km) NW of Wakefield

This community is now, to all intents and purposes, a suburb of the city of Wakefield. A century ago, however, it had its own municipal services and a proud independence founded on textile manufacture and related industries. Pride of place went to **Colbeck's Mill,** a huge place with its own, typical, water source in the form of a dam created from the local beck. For decades the mill produced finest quality worsted cloth, and later the green baize for billiard tables. As with so many other textile interests, it is now closed.

The **church of St Paul** is of robust dimensions, with a particularly prominent tower. It was apparently built during the 1820s with funds provided for church building in rapidly expanding industrial towns and cities following the Battle of Waterloo (1815). Finally aware that Nonconformist groups were increasing their popularity, the Church of England in 1818 set up a society with funds of one million pounds to build new churches; in the 1830s another £500,000 was added to the fund.

A familiar feature of West Yorkshire history is the regular reminders of the price so often paid for coal. In 1973, seven miners working a Lofthouse Colliery seam were killed under Alverthorpe by flooding. There is a memorial to them just off the main road.

ARMLEY [Leeds]

SE2734: 2 miles (3km) W of Leeds

This area on the edge of Leeds city centre was a thriving community in the last century, complete with its own industries and housing for the workers. Today, it has a rather run-down appearance, but possesses one of the most interesting museums of industrial history to be found anywhere.

Armley Mills were built in 1806, and at the time considered to be the biggest such 'manufactory' in Europe. Standing as it does between the River Aire and that 'motorway of commerce' the Leeds-Liverpool Canal, it is easy to see why this textile centre prospered. Now the home of the **Leeds Industrial Museum,** it takes the visitor through the story of the woollen industry in both a local and international context. Exhibits include explanations of the whole production process from sheep's back to finished garment, and there are re-creations of a turn-ofthe-century street and even a picture house of the 1930s. Well worth a family visit!

Far less inviting is the nearby Armley Prison, a sombre, forbidding pile.

ARTHINGTON [Leeds]

4 miles (6km) E of Otley

Not far from the famous **Harewood House,** this small settlement dates back to at least Saxon times. At the Conquest the Saxon 'thane' Alward owned it. A thane was a prominent figure in English social life at the time who held land and the riches it brought by gift of the king. In return, Alward and his predecessors would have had to provide military service when required. Not surprisingly, William of Normandy was happy to dispossess Alward and grant Arthington, and huge tracks of land throughout the kingdom, to his half-brother Robert, Count of Montaine.

The church of St Peter is a typical piece of Gothic Revival by that chief-practitioner of the style – Sir George Gilbert Scott (1864). Sir George was arguably the most influential British architect of the later Victorian period, designing literally hundreds of public and ecclesiastical buildings, including St Pancras Station, the Albert Memorial and Glasgow University.

Dissolved by Henry VIII, Arthington Nunnery was rebuilt in the 1580s and still carries the same name as a private home. A fine example of Elizabethan building styles it boasts a two-storey oriel or 'bay' window above the main door.

BADSWORTH [Wakefield]

SE4615: 2½ miles (4km) NE of Hemsworth

Remarkably, for its location in the middle of an area dominated for a century and more by coal mining, the hamlet of Badsworth remains, in some respects at least, a farming community. Seemingly untouched by the industrial activity just miles away in every direction, the honey-coloured Ackworth sandstone, which makes up its build-

ings, causes it to look more like a village in the Cotswolds than one in West Yorkshire.

This picturesque quality, combined with the age and character of its buildings, means that homes here now command handsome prices and are in great demand. The centrepiece is **the church of St Mary**, a largely Perpendicular construction of the 15th century, but with earlier features. Notable are its four bells, which date back to 1580, a 500-year-old font from **Barnsley Parish Church**, and some of its Victorian stained glass.

The church found a place in the history of the English Civil War when Parliamentarians laid siege to nearby Pontefract Castle. A Badsworth resident of Royalist sympathy is supposed to have removed the fine medieval stained glass and buried it for safekeeping. He was killed in the subsequent fighting and the location of the glass remains a mystery to this day.

Another Civil War figure, Parliamentarian Sir John Bright, the man who accepted the surrender of the King's men at Pontefract in 1644, bought **Badsworth Hall** and estate. The hall was demolished in 1940, but the grand **Old Rectory** still survives, along with many other interesting buildings.

BAILDON [Bradford]

SE1340: 4½ miles (7km) NNW of Bradford

The small town of Baildon has plenty of typical Pennine-style buildings of the 19th century and the early part of the 20th, together with the **church of St John**. Built in 1848 on the site of a much earlier church, history records that the vicar responsible died the day after its reopening. There is some interesting Victorian stained glass and the tower was built in 1928 as a memorial to the town's sons who died in the First World War.

Most visitors will come here to enjoy the area's scenery and walking opportunities. First take a look at the exhibits at **Bracken Hill Countryside Centre** on Glen Road. There are static displays and interactive exhibits on the natural history, geology and archaeology of **Shipley Glen**. There are demonstrations on a range of subjects and regular talks, walks and activity days for young and old alike.

Not far away is a stone circle known as **Soldier's Trench** and thought to date back 3000 years to the Bronze Age. Indeed, this whole area and neighbouring **Ilkley Moor**, still echo of a pagan past, which today is hard to interpret. **Baildon Moor,** handsome walking country high above the valley, is made even more interesting by the presence of outcropping gritstones carved with 'cup and ring' designs. What they mean, we will never know for certain; they could be of ceremonial origin, simple boundary stones, or once-popular early Bronze Age graffiti.

BARDSEY [Leeds]

SE3643: 7½ miles (12km) NNE of Leeds

More correctly known as Bardsey-cum-Rigton, to link it with its sibling settlement of **East Rigton** on the other side of the A58, it has two major claims to fame. The first is its ancient **church of All Hallows**, which displays an Anglo-Saxon tower, albeit with Perpendicular additions. It also has remarkable zigzag and dog-tooth features charting ecclesiastical architecture through the Norman and Early English periods and beyond. The second is Bardsey's pub. The Bingley Arms has earned its place in the Guinness Book of Records as England's oldest pub, with a record of innkeepers dating back to more than a century before the Conquest. The middle section of the building can be dated back to that time and comes complete with a pair of priest's holes; the remainder was added in the 18th century.

Both the inn and the village as a whole were, in medieval times, a 'grange' or sheep farm holding belonging to the monks of **Kirkstall Abbey.** It was established by them in the 12th century and joined many others in an industry which made monasteries rich and English wool the staple textile of Western Europe well into the late medieval period.

Archaeologists believe the village's Castle Hill was the site of a motte and bailey construction in the 1100s but nothing much remains of it today.

You can't blame a place for claiming a famous son, and Bardsey does so by virtue of the fact that the playwright William

Congreve was born at Bardsey Grange in 1670 because his mother was travelling through the area when he decided to enter the world. Famous for his satirical works, particularly *Love for Love* and *Way of the World*, Congreve was educated at Trinity College, Dublin and never returned to his birthplace. Cataracts blinded him while still relatively young and he died in a coach crash – there were road hogs around even in those days. Bardsey's loss was literature's gain and the great man was buried in Westminster Abbey.

BARWICK-IN-ELMET [Leeds]

SE3937: 6 miles (10km) NNE of Leeds

Without doubt the best known feature of this village is its magnificent maypole. In ancient times, when the seasons meant everything to agricultural communities – rather than the occasional inconveniences of today, nature and the worship of the elements and their creations were highly significant. Even with the coming of Christianity, certain traditions, including collecting a living tree from the wildwood and 'worshipping' it with due reverence continued. In past centuries, May Day celebrations were joyous, noisy, and rowdy affairs. Although maypole dancing has all but disappeared, it is still going strong in Barwick. The pole, all 90ft of it, stands tall all year round in the village square. Every three years, on Easter Monday, it is lowered with great cere-

mony, repaired and redecorated before a crowd of thousands – get there early for a good view.

Other interesting features include a motte and bailey mound of Norman origin – **Hall Tower Hill** – and the **church of All Saints.** The latter is mainly of the 14th century but has a (disputed) Decorated vestry door from about 100 years earlier.

BATLEY [Kirklees]

SE2424: 2 miles (3km) S of Dewsbury

There will be some for whom the Batley Variety Club, that fulcrum of chicken in the basket culture of the 1970s, is all that springs to mind when this steady West Yorkshire town is mentioned. But think again, because in the last century this was one of a large number of prosperous industrial centres which made a few rich and gave employment and security, albeit not particularly well-paid, to thousands.

Much of what we see today, particularly the once cobbled streets of terraced houses, dates from Victorian times when Batley was centre of the 'shoddy' trade. A 'green' industry 150 years before its time, the shoddy trade recycled the wool in rags and old clothes into a state in which they could be rewoven to make blankets, carpets, military uniforms and other heavy woollen products. It led to grand buildings, including the homes of some of the 'shoddy barons'. These included Benjamin Law, the 'Shoddy King' of nearby Birstall who is buried in **Batley Cemetery.**

The mainly 15th-century **church of All Saints** was the centre of religious devotion until the 1800s and is worth a visit for its interesting alabaster tomb of Sir Richard Mirfield and his wife (dated 1496). But by the 19th century Methodism had well and truly taken root in this bustling town, and the remarkable **'Shoddy Temple'** or **Zionist Chapel**, in the central square justifies a visit on its own. Dated to 1869, at the height of 'shoddy' prosperity, it gained its nickname from the belief that more business deals were struck on its steps after Sunday service than during the rest of the working week.

Another monument to textile triumphalism is the **Bagshaw Museum** in Batley's attractive **Wilton Park.** This marvellous building was once the private home of a tycoon – it now contains exhibits charting the history of the area, together with more eclectic items from the Orient and Ancient Egypt.

Batley still retains its cobbled market place, a robust town hall and a highly respected grammar school founded in 1612. The latter can list among its old boys Sir Titus Salt, the hugely wealthy industrialist, and Joseph Priestley, who combined a career in the church with a lifelong interest in the sciences. Born in 1733, he was a friend of the American Revolutionary politician Benjamin Franklin, the potter Josiah Wedgwood, and was even invited to accompany Captain James Cook on his first voyage of discovery (he declined). Mixing science with religion was unpopular in 18th-century England and Priestley was branded an atheist. He eventually emigrated to America where his free-thinking was more positively received. He is widely credited with being one of the discoverers of oxygen.

BEN RHYDDING [Bradford]

SE1247: 1 mile (2km) E of Ilkley

This settlement might at first glance be mistaken for little more than an extension of nearby Ilkley. In fact, it was and is a village in its own right, and until the latter half of the last century it was known as Wheatley. Wheatley Hall, a private residence built in the 1670s, still stands.

It was in 1844 that the fortunes of Wheatley changed to usher in a period of relative prosperity. In 1844, local entrepreneur Hamer Stansfield took a 'water cure' in Germany and was so impressed by the efficacy of the treatment that he decided to adopt the idea here. The first 'hydropathic' centre in the country, named the Ben Rhydding Hydropathic Hotel, was built above the village and attracted the Victorian era's most well-to-do clients. A station was built in 1865, specifically to take rail passengers to the Hydro, and the place provided valued employment to a good number of local people. Trends and fashions change and eventually the building was turned over to other uses, before disappearing altogether half a century ago.

BIRDSEDGE [Wakefield]

SE2007: 4 miles (6km) NW of Penistone

Sitting on the 1000ft contour, this must be one of the highest villages in the locality, an area well known for high villages. Little more than the site of a couple of farms three centuries ago, Birdsedge grew up when a major toll road built by John Metcalf (known as 'Blind Jack of Knaresborough') came through the area, linking Huddersfield and Barnsley in 1825.

Prior to that, a community of Quakers had established themselves in the 17th century, and both here and in nearby Penistone, there are still reminders of their influence in buildings and burial grounds.

The main employment, apart from farming, was provided by a woollen mill founded about 200 years ago and powered by the waters of the infant River Dearne. The mill is still in use and serves as a well-preserved reminder of how these smaller factories, soon superseded in many larger towns by much bigger establishments, would have looked.

BINGLEY [Bradford]

SE1039: 5½ miles (9km) NW of Bradford

If you want a classic 'Airedale' town, then this must be it. The dramatic moorland scenery near at hand combines effortlessly with the compact development that came with industrialisation. A textile town like its many neighbours, Bingley came to prominence when the builders of the Leeds and Liverpool Canal decided to cut their way across the Pennines via the Aire Gap.

At 127 miles long the canal, begun in 1770 but not completed until 1816, is the longest in England and cost almost one million pounds when built – a colossal sum for the time. As a motor for economic revolution it has no equal, linking the cotton and engineering centres of the north-west with the woollen and minerals industries of Yorkshire, it was always going to be successful. Not all things went smoothly though, particularly around Bingley where the builders were forced to construct a three-tier, and then the magnificent **Five Rise Lock**. The latter, just on the edge of the town, is signposted and reached by a pleasant walk along the canal towpath.

Dating from the same period, and in the town proper, the **town hall** was once a private home, known as Myrtle Grove; hence **Myrtle Park** in which it stands. The path extends down to the river and the ancient, stone **Beckfoot** packhorse bridge at **Harden Beck**.

The mainly Tudor **church of All Saints** is worth visiting, perhaps most of all for its Burne-Jones window made in 1873. Sir Edward Coley Burne-Jones was a friend and business partner of the great Pre-Raphaelite designer and artist

William Morris and took his subjects from Greek and Arthurian mythology, often with the greatest possible creative licence. Buried in the churchyard is John Nicholson, known affectionately as 'the Airedale poet' for his romantic verses in Wordsworthian style proclaiming the beauty of this area. He began his career in roguish fashion, as did Wordsworth, with an all-consuming passion for the good things in life. Unlike Wordsworth, however, (he probably didn't have a sister Dorothy nagging him at home) he carried on his drinking hobby, married several times and spent large sums of money. Unfortunately, though with splendid irony, he ended his days in 1843 when – after a substantial skinful – he slipped from stepping stones, into the Aire and drowned.

Next to the church is the 16th-century **White Hart Inn,** with its mullioned windows a rare reminder that there was a time before terraced houses and woollen mills.

BIRSTALL [Kirklees]

SE2226: 3 miles (5km) NNW of Dewsbury

Just down the road from Batley, this is a pleasant enough township. The **church of St Peter** boasts a Norman tower and an interesting brass memorial showing an Elizabeth Popeley in an open shroud with her daughters kneeling beside her. In the graveyard, we find Ellen Nussey and Margaret Wooler, both friends of novelist Charlotte Brontë.

And it is the famous writer who makes a visit to Birstall especially worthwhile. On Nutter Lane, just off the A652, is **Oakwell Hall and Country Park.** What a gem this is: built in 1583 it is a marvellous example of an Elizabethan manor house set in its own grounds. There is fine oak panelling, mullioned windows, decorated plaster ceilings and a Great Hall with gallery. The place is made much more interesting by its decorations and furniture, which are contemporary with its ownership by the Batt family in the 1690s. There is an authentic Stuart herb garden and 100 acres in which to walk or take part in one of the organised natural history events.

Charlotte Brontë visited Oakwell in the 1840s and used it as the basis for Fieldhead, the home of her heroine in her novel *Shirley,* set amid the Luddite risings.

BOSTON SPA [Leeds]

SE4245: 2 miles (3km) S of Wetherby

This genteel and attractive town stands on the banks of the River Wharfe and owes its beauty and one-time prosperity to a certain John Shires. In 1744 Shires discovered that a combination of magnesian limestone and sulphur springs produced just the kind of foul-smelling waters which were so much in vogue in other parts of the country and on the Continent.

The place, then and until the middle of the last century known as **Thorp Spa,** attracted fine gentlemen and ladies by the coach-load, all eager to partake of the healing water cures and gossip the season away. Although the spa was finally eclipsed by the facilities and attractions offered not far away in Harrogate, the fine Georgian buildings on **High Street** bear testament to the thriving place it must once have been.

BOWLING [Bradford]

SE1732: 1 mile (2km) SE of Bradford

Now no more than a suburb of Bradford, Bowling had an individual identity by virtue of the fact that it grew up around **Bolling Hall**, a medieval house with a host of later additions. Together the mixture of architectural styles combine to make the house worth a few hours of anybody's time and it is open all year round.

Bolling Hall's oldest element is a medieval tower, to which a magnificent front was added in the 17th century. Later owners altered and fiddled to add rooms and features of great character. The modern visitor is able to look at rooms decorated and furnished as they would have been during episodes in the hall's history, from Tudor times to the fashionable Regency period. Don't miss the room devoted to the 'Bradford Pals' Regiment – wiped out along with so many others comprised of friends from the same town at the Battle of the Somme in 1916.

Needless to say, a house of this age comes with its own mysterious stories and tales, including the mystery of the bloodstain on one floor and the famous ghost. The latter, in the shape of a woman, is reputed to have appeared to the Earl of Newcastle while he rested at Bolling Hall on the eve of the Royalist assault on Bradford in 1643. Apparently, the citizens of Bradford feared a massacre, and the ghost woke up the slumbering Earl and shrieked 'pity poor Bradford' three times. Needless to say, the town was taken, but without the carnage the locals had feared. All tosh, of course, but would you spend the night there? Bolling Hall is signed off the A650 out of Bradford city centre.

BRADFORD [Bradford]

SE1633: 12½ miles (20km) NNW of Huddersfield

Bradford is one of Yorkshire's most important cities – arguably the most important truly 'industrialised' city in the county and one of the most important in the north of England. Plenty of guides exist on this one city alone, and here we can't attempt to capture everything it has to offer. Instead, what follows is an overview of a city that rewards several visits or perhaps a weekend involving a stay at one of its fine hotels.

Until the end of the 18th century, Bradford was just another small woollen and market town in a fold of the Pennine hills. It was prosperous enough, and well known for the quality of its fine woollen textiles, but it differed little from Huddersfield, and was nowhere near as large or important a trading centre as Leeds, Halifax or Wakefield. During the English Civil War it was a Parliamentary stronghold which twice underwent Royalist siege, but it was not until the coming of steam and the revolution in manufacturing that it took centre stage. In 1801 the town's population – for Bradford was then still very much a town – was a mere 6400. Half a century later it had soared to just over 100,000 and by 1881 it was 183,000. A mere 20 years later, when Queen Victoria died, it had reached an incredible 280,000. Despite the growth in the number of mills and houses in which the workers lived, no urban centre could grow at such a rate without massive social disruption. There were huge demands on sanitation and other public services, and an extremely young population needed a large education service.

All this means that the Bradford we see today – if possible doing so without the ring roads and other monstrosities of the 1960s and '70s – is essentially a Victorian city. One firm of architects, Lockwood and Mawson, were responsible for a large number of public buildings and stamped their stylish, Italianate mark both here and at **Saltaire** a few miles away.

Although much added to in the 19th century, one of Bradford's oldest buildings is the **Cathedral**. Until 1919 this was the parish church of St Peter and was built, naturally

enough considering the surrounding hills, of millstone grit. Much of the building dates from the 14th century and is of the Perpendicular style; despite considerable Victorian alteration the interior retains a pleasing and successful medieval feel. The west tower was built at the beginning of the 16th century and remains one of Bradford's landmarks due to its prominent position above the heart of the city proper. Inside, the magnificent 15th-century font cover is very fine and provides interesting comparison with that at Halifax. Notable, too, are the stained-glass windows in the chancel, which represent some of the earliest work of Morris & Co. Experts reckon they see the skills of Ford Madox Brown, Rossetti and Burne-Jones, the three giants of the Arts and Crafts Movement which took the creative world by storm in the second half of the 19th century. A monument of particular interest is that to Joseph Priestley, engineer of the Leeds and Liverpool Canal – and one of the reasons for Bradford's huge industrial growth when it arrived here in 1774. His grave bears a scale model of the waterway under construction.

Bradford has numerous other churches, but one especially worth a look is **the parish church of All Saints** on Little Horton Green. Built in 1864, this is the grandest Victorian church in the city and boasts a delicate spire and a highly unusual brass and iron pulpit.

Other public buildings of special

note include the magnificent **St George's Hall** which was built in 1853 by Lockwood and Mawson and to this day plays host to conferences and musical concerts. The same firm of architects was also responsible for two other major buildings, namely the **town hall** (1873) and the **Wool Exchange** on Market Street. This latter was built between 1864-7 and, better than any other, celebrates the wealth and power of Bradford when it dominated the world's woollen textile production. All the great social reformers and industrialists of the age are celebrated here, including Cobden, Salt, Watt and Arkwright. A wander around the relatively compact city centre reveals other stunning buildings, including the ostentatiously decorated merchant halls and warehouses of '**Little Germany**' close to the Cathedral. Try the heritage walk around this area, named after the German traders who came to the town and opened up commercial routes with their home country and the rest of the continent. Among them was the father of composer Frederick Delius. Also in this area is the unique **Colour Museum** on Providence Street. Established by the Society of Dyers and Colourists, this is both a celebration of the creativity of colour in textiles, and an excellent educational attraction for youngsters, giving them a literal eye-witness view of how different animals see colours, and what it is like to be colour blind.

Across the city is the **Alhambra Theatre**, built in Edwardian times and recently restored to play host to the world's finest touring companies. Nearby is a statue to Bradford-born author J.B. (John Boynton) Priestley. His *The Good Companions* hilariously sums up both the generosity – and the pomposity – of characters in his hometown. Just above the statue to the great novelist and playwright is the **National Museum of Photography, Film and Television**. This justly famous centre of the visual arts has just been given a complete and thorough overhaul and now includes the world's biggest IMAX film studio.

Other museums worth visiting include the **Cartwright Hall** in Lister Park. The building houses important collections of 19th- and early 20th-century paintings, including many Pre-Raphaelites, together with more recent artists including Bradford's own David Hockney.

While Bradford has plenty to offer the amateur historian, particularly one interested in the rise and fall of Britain's industrial heritage, it has other attractions too. Before and after the Second World War large numbers of people from the Indian subcontinent came here to work in the mills and in other labour-intensive jobs. Now very much a vital part of the Bradford scene, this community has brought with it its exciting culture, and its wonderful cuisine. Bradford has some of the finest **curry houses** in Europe – and some of the best Asian supermarkets. If ever you need an ingredient for that special recipe, you will get it here!

BRAMHAM [Leeds]

SE4343: 2 miles (3km) S of Boston Spa

Close to the Great North Road, the village of Bramham has some lovely stone houses dating from the 18th century and the **church of All Saints**, with its Norman tower topped by a Perpendicular spire, is worth looking at. Of special interest is the unusual early 20th-century panelling and screen in the chancel.

Nearby is **Bramham Park**, one of the most impressive and important examples of Queen Anne architecture in the country. Built around 1700 in the French classical style for Lord Bingley, who became the Queen's Lord Chamberlain, it has been likened to Versailles in its proportions and its magnificent gardens. Architectural historian Nikolaus Pevsner, never one to pay a compliment if he didn't have to, said of it, 'If ever house and gardens must be regarded as one ensemble, it is here. Bramham is a grand and unusual house, but its gardens are grander and even more unusual.'

The reason, apparently, is that while elsewhere the influences of Capability Brown and his followers helped do away with such designs, here they survived. Along with Hampton Court, they are said to be the finest examples of Louis XIV-style gardens in the country, complete with canals, long avenues, cascades and statues. The house itself is full of furniture and other valuable decorations, together with portraits by, among others, Sir Joshua Reynolds.

BRAMHOPE [Leeds]

SE2543: 4 miles (6km) E of Otley

This village, now a popular residence for those who work in nearby Leeds, stands at the entrance to Wharfedale and the Yorkshire Dales proper. Perhaps not surprisingly, the area was until this century dominated by agriculture, with the focal point of village life being the doings of those in charge at **Bramhope Hall.** The building has now gone but in its grounds, and built by Robert Dyneley, the owner in 1649, is the **Puritan Chapel.** This building is of major historical significance and represents one of the earliest forms of architecture of this kind with its simple basic format and plain design.

Particularly interesting is the three-tier pulpit, faced by box pews that gave the worshippers no opportunity whatsoever to avoid the gaze of their blood and thunder preacher. The word 'Puritan' was applied to that collection of Nonconformist Christian groupings that felt the Reformation of the English Church under Queen Elizabeth had not gone far enough. They took the Bible and its literal teachings as the only true guide to living their lives and espoused all ancient traditions and customs – not a fun-loving bunch, by anybody's standards.

BRIESTFIELD [Kirklees]

SE2317: 4 miles (6km) W of Horbury

This tiny village up on the 'tops' above Dewsbury must have been a desolate place before improvements in transportation. Not surprisingly, perhaps, along with struggling to make a living from hill farming – always a precarious existence, right up to the present day – some families had handloom weaving frames in the third storey of their homes. Here the whole family would toil away, especially in winter, turning wool into lengths of cloth for sale in neighbouring towns. A wander around the village shows up several of these houses.

Understandably, as bigger and more efficient machines were developed at the start of the 19th century, forcing workers into large factories, the handloom weavers of this part of Yorkshire (together with those in Lancashire, Nottinghamshire and Cheshire) saw their precarious living under threat. Local tradition has it that some of those who tried, in vain, to stop the drive to modernity – the Luddites – came from Briestfield. Named after the fictional leader 'Ned Ludd', the Luddites embarked on a campaign of machine-breaking in the years 1811 to 1816.

Inevitably, the rule of law was finally re-established, with many being imprisoned or transported. They might not have prevented the 'factory system' but their protests against poor wages and terrible factory conditions did force some concessions from mill owners.

BRIGHOUSE [Calderdale]

SE1423: 4 miles (6km) ESE of Halifax

The name of this typical Pennine town is believed to come from the fact that a building will almost certainly have stood on, or very close to, the **bridge** which crossed the River Calder at this point. Once the river had been bridged at great local expense, travellers were charged to cross – with the consequent need for an attendant on hand to take fees.

What is certain is that Brighouse's history has been dominated by the river, first as source of power for the flour milling which still provides local employment, and then in the last century for the textile mills which sprang up by its banks. The key to Brighouse's growth at the end of the 18th century was the development of the **Calder and Hebble Navigation**. In 1757 engineer John Smeaton set about providing a serviceable navigable waterway between Wakefield and Halifax, using rivers where suitable and then cutting canals between them to centres of population and industry. It wasn't finished until 1770. The **canal basin** is an interesting spot from which to set out on a walk and the waterway can be followed, via its towpath, from here to Sowerby Bridge nearly eight miles away.

The town centre is mainly pedestrianised and has an interesting pub *The Prince of Wales*. It looks ancient, but dates back to the 1920s and is constructed from the timbers of an old sailing ship.

Both of Brighouse's churches date from the last century, indicating the growth in the population. Both **St Martin's Church** and **St James's Church** contain excellent stained glass from the Morris factory. The latter's glass was designed by no less a trio than Dante Gabriel Rossetti, Madox Brown and Burne-Jones.

Near the town centre, on Halifax Road, is the **Smith Art Gallery**. It houses a fine collection of Victorian paintings.

BROCKHOLES [Kirklees]

SE1411: 3 miles (5km) S of Huddersfield

Driving through this small town on the road between Huddersfield and Holmfirth, it is easy to see why the place got its name as the 'domain of the badger'. The River Holme has cut its way through the valley and tree-clad slopes above the houses give the area a closed-in feel.

The mills that once provided work for local people have now gone, but some of the homes specially built to house the workers are still there. A local historian has written of an 18th-century vicar of Holmfirth who decided to eke out his living by clipping coins; he was caught and executed for his trouble – but his son got a job at the Royal Mint!

BURLEY-IN-WHARFEDALE [Leeds]

SE1645: 4 miles (6km) W of Otley

This is a pleasant village on the road into Wharfedale and quite unlike many more 'typical' West Yorkshire textile towns. But textile town it once was, with first cotton and later woollen worsted mills by the banks of the river. Interestingly, the main place of employment, **Greenholme,** was designed to fit into the local landscape rather than destroy it. Orphans from London and other large cities were recruited to work here and made their lives in the community. The mill later had Liberal Quaker politician William Forster as one of its owners. Although born in Dorset he considered this area his home and was MP for Bradford for many years. A member of the Cabinet, he was responsible for the great Elementary Education Act of 1870, and under Gladstone became Chief Secretary for Ireland. He is buried in the yard of **St Mary's Church**.

Another famous son is Sir William Watson, the popular Victorian poet who wrote a collection of works paying tribute to the great masters of his art, including Wordsworth.

CALVERLEY [Leeds]

SE2036: 4½ miles (7km) NE of Bradford

Positioned on one of the main roads linking Leeds and Bradford, it is not surprising that the township of Calverley now attracts residents who find their work in one of these two great cities. A century ago it was a different story, with a number of woollen mills providing employment for the inhabitants.

One reason to visit Calverley today is the **church of St Wilfrid**, a large structure with some Norman remnants but largely of the early 13th-century Decorated style and therefore rather uncommon in this area. Look out for the piscina, a kind of stone sink used to dispose of Holy Water into consecrated ground, and a familiar feature in churches of this age. The intricate Jacobean font cover is also worthy of note.

Most interesting of all for those with a fascination for the macabre and unexplained is the story of Walter Calverley of **Calverley Old Hall**. The tale goes that in 1604 the aforementioned Lord of the Manor, having squandered his inheritance, finally cracked under the strain and murdered two of his children, and left his wife for dead. He then set out on horseback to slay his infant son who was being cared for elsewhere by a nurse. The horse threw the murderer, and he was captured and taken to York for trial. Unwilling to plead, therefore allowing his surviving son to inherit his property, he was punished by being pressed to death. The story has it that he begged for an end to his agony by pleading, 'A pund more weight! Lig on, lig on!'

Needless to say, after all this trauma and infamy the ghost of Walter Calverley is still said to haunt the Old Hall brandishing a bloodstained knife; others claim to have seen him riding his horse in the nearby countryside. Whether true or not, it was once taken seriously enough to be the subject of a church sanctioned exorcism – which failed. The story, known as *The Yorkshire Tragedy*, was once spuriously attributed to Shakespeare.

CAPHOUSE COLLIERY [Wakefield]

SE2517: 4miles (6km) SW of Wakefield

At the edge of the tiny village of **Overton**, this is the place those wanting to know more about the history of coal mining should visit. Crucially important in the economic and social development of West Yorkshire, coal has as much a part to play in the county's history as the textile industry. It created its own communities, informed the local psyche, and when it died caused untold damage which has yet to be repaired.

Caphouse Colliery was one of scores in West Yorkshire but, unlike almost all its neighbours, on closure as a working mine was given a new life. An ambitious scheme created what is now, rather wordily, the **National Coal Mining Museum for England,** complete with visitor centre and pit-top displays of machinery from the basic items used centuries ago to the high-tech equipment of today. But what sets Caphouse apart is the chance to go underground and see first-hand what it must have been like to toil for a lifetime in the damp, dark and dangerous world of the coal mine.

Visitors don safety helmets and lamps, then hand in their 'tally' (a numbered disc for ensuring all those who go down the pit come up again) before stepping into the lift, or 'cage', for a journey 450ft down to the pit bottom. Here, guided by an experienced former miner, visitors see how the job developed from the days when children worked the coal to the modern era. Once underground, it doesn't take much imagination to see why men still die in mining accidents – and why so many were killed in days gone by.

The colliery dates from the late 18th century and was operated by the Lister-Kaye family from nearby Denby Grange for much of the succeeding centuries. The museum recently re-opened the underground workings, following water inundation, thanks to a large Lottery Fund allocation.

CARR GATE [Wakefield]

SE3124: 2 miles (4km) NW of Wakefield

Located on the edge of Wakefield, this community stands on ground which once flooded regularly thanks to the low-lying nature of the land. There are many 'carrs' in this region, a word traceable back to Old Norse and meaning marshy or boggy ground. Of interest is the Elim Pentecostalist Church residential home at **Melbourne House**, built in the last century by a very wealthy prophet-style religious fanatic for his followers.

CASTLEFORD [Wakefield]

SE4525: 2½ miles (4km) NNW of Pontefract

With typical lack of sympathy, the great chronicler of British architecture Sir Nikolaus Pevsner, in his *Buildings of England* says of Castleford, 'There does not seem to be a single building in the centre of town which would justify mention.' It is true that regular development and redevelopment in the last two centuries have removed much of the traces of the town's past, but it is a past which is still traceable in the history books and worth exploring.

Since time immemorial, a settlement at this natural fording of the River Aire must have played host to man. Soon after the Emperor Claudius landed in Britain in AD43 the legions began to move north, eventually constructing the Great North Road to York. Just over 20 miles south of the great Roman centre, Castleford was an ideal site for a legionary garrison based in a defended fort with a civilian population housed outside. As with military bases across the Roman world, the fort at Castleford came complete with stables, a hospital, granaries and, closer to the river, a bathhouse. Although nothing of 'Legioleum', or Roman Castleford, can now be seen in-situ, both the town **museum** and that at Wakefield house artefacts.

When the legions left, Anglo-Saxon settlers arrived and probably still used the Roman ford across the Aire, thus giving us

'Caester Forda' and, ultimately, the modern appellation.

Once a quiet country village, everything changed with the arrival of the Industrial Revolution and its factories, mines, canals and railways. Records show a staggering rise in population, from 890 in 1811 to 14,143 in 1891, many of them working in mines, thousands more in glass-making and chemicals – industries for which the town is still known.

Castleford's most famous son is probably the late Henry Moore, the son of a local miner. He studied at Leeds and the Royal College of Art and became one of the most influential and important sculptors of his time. His work is familiar for its stylised recreation of the human form, usually in larger-than-life scale, and graces important buildings and public places all over the world. Leeds City Art Gallery has one of Moore's works at its entrance and there are several at the **Yorkshire Sculpture Park** at Bretton.

Yorkshire Sculpture Park

CLAYTON WEST [Wakefield]

SE2511: 3 miles (5km) E of Denby Dale

This small village is remarkable as the home of the **Kirklees Light Railway.** Ever fancied a toy railway? Well, this is an example of taking your hobby a step too far; the dream of a local entrepreneur and, inevitably, railway fan, who brought an old branch line back to life by laying a 15-inch (38cm) narrow gauge line on the old trackbed.

Visitors, and children in particular, love this attraction and travel eight miles to a junction with the Huddersfield-Sheffield line via a quarter-mile tunnel. The steam locomotives have been hand-built by the volunteers and enthusiasts who keep the place going. There are miniature trains at the station, together with a shop and café. A grand way to spend a Sunday afternoon.

CLECKHEATON [Bradford]

SE1924: 5½ miles (9km) SSE of Bradford

This small town is another which has suffered over recent decades from the decline in the all-powerful textile industry, although it still retains its popular markets on Tuesdays and Saturdays. Significant public buildings are hard to come by, but the **White Chapel**, a church of 1831, is interesting for some of its decorations. Previous ecclesiastical buildings have stood on the same site, and buried here is Richard Richardson, an 18th-century physician and more besides. A friend of the great naturalist Sir Hans Sloane, he travelled the country in search of botanical specimens; word has it that he had the second 'hothouse' in England.

For those in any doubt as to the foul air and general pollution towns such as this suffered in the Industrial Revolution, consider the following saying citing Cleckheaton as the place where, 'T' ducks fly back'ards ter keep t'muck aht o' the'r een'. A number of other towns, including Pudsey and Dewsbury, had the same saying. In Sheffield it was said that 'even t'sparrers wake up coughin''.

CLIFFORD [Leeds]

SE4244: 4 miles (6km) SSE of Wetherby

This quiet Wharfedale village, not far from **Boston Spa**, might attract few casual visitors were it not for its magnificent **church of St Edward**. This Roman Catholic edifice is a true work of genius, built between 1845-8 to the design of a young Scots architect named Ramsay. Nikolaus Pevsner writes of Ramsey touring Europe, studying architecture and drawing his own 'ideal' church. A Yorkshire gentleman on a shooting tour in Scotland later bought that design – for £50. True or no, it is a good story, and one worthy of such a marvellous building with a stupendous west tower.

Built by the local Grimston family, who had a flax mill in Clifford, they received grants from the Pope and a collection of European monarchs. The design is Romanesque. Inside, look for the beautiful statue of the Virgin by K. Hofmann, a Jew from Rome who was so moved by his creation he converted to Catholicism. Look out too for four windows by Englishman August Pugin, a founder of the Arts and Crafts Movement and close friend of John Ruskin.

COLLINGHAM [Leeds]

SE3845: 2½ miles (4km) SSW of Wetherby

Standing on the River Wharfe, Collingham has an interesting history with evidence of human habitation hereabouts dating back at least to the Iron Age. Just outside the village, at **Dalton Parlours**, antiquarians in the last century uncovered what is believed to have been a **Roman villa**. Of particular importance was a **mosaic pavement** with a head of Medusa in the design. In addition, artefacts were found linking the building to the Sixth Legion, which arrived at the time of Emperor Hadrian and stayed in the area for 300 years.

Positioned as it is, on a major route north, it is not surprising invading Romans walked this way, nor that highwayman Dick Turpin is said to have stayed at the **Old Starr** pub

In the village, the **church of St Oswald** has elements dating back to Norman times with, remarkably, some masonry from the Saxon period. Especially interesting are fragments of Saxon crosses, including one – the **Apostle's Cross** with designs placing it in the 8th century and representations of the Apostles from the 800s up the sides.

Not surprising then, considering the village's age, that there are a number of spooky and bloodthirsty stories attached to Collingham. The most gruesome must be that of the 'Collingham Robbers' who, in 1674, are supposed to have robbed the richest man in Yorkshire. They had their horses shod back to front so that their tracks would confuse those in pursuit. As in all the best detective stories, it didn't work out because their dog was left at the scene of the crime, only to return home later, along with officers of the law.

The pair were hanged for their crime, but their apprentice was reportedly forced to carry out the punishment. Perhaps not surprisingly, the story concludes with the poor lad so traumatised by his duty that he throttled himself with the same rope. Whether it is the apprentice, the robbers, or some other troubled soul, there is a history of sightings of apparitions in the area.

COPLEY [Calderdale]

SE0822: 2 miles (3km) S of Halifax

The historian of the Industrial Revolution will have to make a pilgrimage to this small settlement, if only on the grounds that it was the site of one of the first attempts by a mill owner in Yorkshire to provide not only a place of employment, but also one of residence, worship and amusement – in short, a whole community predating Sir Titus Salt's Saltaire near Bradford.

Woollen magnate Colonel Edward Ackroyd built a mill here in 1847, with houses for the workforce and a school and library for their education. There was a canteen, where hundreds of workers were served dinners for a penny-ha'penny and, inevitably via a bridge across the River Calder, the **church of St Stephen.** The building is large and plain, but with a large bell tower at the west end.

CRIGGLESTONE [Wakefield]

SE3116: 2 miles (4km) S of Wakefield

This small community is not one but several small hamlets. All once independent communities, they are now to all intents and purposes combined. The locality bears all the familiar scars of the last 200 years of industrial rise and fall, together with the M1 that carved through its middle. The coking tips that once marred the area are gone, and now many choose to live here and work in Wakefield or Leeds.

CROFTON [Wakefield]

SE3717: 4 miles (6km) ESE of Wakefield

This is a pleasant village, with the **church of All Saints** providing an excellent reason to spend an hour or so exploring. Cruciform in shape, with no aisles, it is unusual in that the whole building was constructed in one go, in the first quarter of the 15th century. Evidence points to the fact that it was built under orders from Bishop Fleming of Lincoln, who was born in the hamlet of Crofton. There must have been a church here before, however, as the visitor can also take in two **Saxon crosses,** one carved with the likeness of a bishop, the other of entwined beasts.

DARRINGTON [Wakefield]

SE4820: 2 miles (3km) SE of Pontefract

In one direction are Castleford, Pontefract and the other towns which 150 years ago were transformed by 'progress' into mining communities; in the other there are the rural settlements of Ackworth, Wentbridge and Badsworth. Happily for those who live there, Darrington, like the three latter villages, was lucky enough to avoid the worst excesses of the Industrial Revolution. Surviving as an agricultural centre, providing produce for Pontefract market, just as it had for the past 1000 years Darrington let mechanisation pass it by.

Until the second half of the 20th century it maintained its rural employment with local people working on neighbouring farms and estates. One odd crop was teasels, grown for the woollen industry to the west of the county and used to raise the nap on cloth for finishing. The plant was 'phased out' by the middle of the 19th century when machines replaced it.

The principal building in the village, raised slightly above it on a slope, is the **church of St Luke and All Saints.** It boasts a Norman tower with a unique 14th-century rood-stair turret leading to a watching gallery. Built in Tadcaster magnesian limestone, the church is worth an exploration for its interesting misericords, carved bench ends and monuments. In the north and south aisle are stone monuments to a 14th-century knight and his lady. It is believed the mailed knight is Sir Waren de Scargil who is thought to have taken part in the Battle of Bannockburn. The churchyard has an interesting **dovecote** dated to the 1700s.

DENBY [Kirklees]

SE2207: 2 miles (4km) N of Penistone

This catch-all name for the two interlinked villages of Upper and Lower Denby dates back to the Domesday Book as the 'place of the Danes' – in other words one which has been occupied and farmed for well over a millennia. Apart from the inevitable quota of new homes and barn and farm conversions, Denby is still an agricultural community, high in the Pennine hills, and with grand views to Emley in one direction and the market town of Penistone in the other.

Many of the **farm buildings** date back, at least in part, to the 16th and 17th centuries and it is easy to see why its isolation led to the well-documented beliefs that over the years a number of witches had lived in the area. Amazingly, one is recorded as living in Denby in the 19th century!

DENBY DALE [Kirklees]

SE2208: 3 miles (5km) N of Penistone

If Denby Dale, now a seemingly endless ribbon development on the Wakefield-Huddersfield road, is known for anything it must be its famous giant meat and potato pies. These creations, the first of which was made in 1788 to celebrate the recovery of King George III from one of his many bouts of mental illness, have got bigger over the years – but rarely stray from controversy. There have been nine Denby Dale Pies in all, the second was made in 1815 to celebrate the defeat of Napoleon, another in 1846 to celebrate the repeal of the Corn Laws and one in 1887 for the Golden Jubilee of Queen Victoria. Unfortunately for all concerned, this particular culinary masterpiece went bad while being baked – presumably a roguish butcher was to blame – and had to be buried in a lime pit, so foul was its stench. The biggest pie yet was baked in 1988, to commemorate the bicentenary of the first one, and provided 40,000 portions. The container it was baked in now contains flowers and stands outside, you guessed it, the **Denby Dale Pie Hall.**

More impressive even than the pies is the marvellous Victorian **railway viaduct** at the western end of the town, which carries the Penistone Line. This superb route is still open, linking travellers between Barnsley and Huddersfield on what must be one of the most spectacular series of viaducts in the region. Ride it at least once and marvel at the skill, ingenuity and downright cheek of our 19th-century forefathers.

DEWSBURY [Kirklees]

SE2422: 6 miles (10km) W of Wakefield

This busy and still important town stands in the heart of the once very important 'shoddy' industry. Here old woollen items were re-used, mixed with new wool and turned into heavy products such as blankets and military uniforms. It was an industry that provided employment for many and made more than a few rich – some of the buildings the latter endowed still give the town its gritty but welcoming character.

Long pre-dating the shoddy era, the **Minster Church of All Saints** once held sway over one of the largest parishes in the north of England; at 400 square miles it stretched to the Lancashire border. It is reputed that St Paulinus began the conversion of the area on the site in 627, using the River Calder to baptise his converts. Paulinus was a Roman Christian missionary who came to England in 601 with St Augustine and became the first Archbishop of York before pagan hordes finally forced him to retreat south.

The bulk of the building is 13th century but, almost inevitably in these parts, much additional work was done in the Victorian era to 'improve' its appearance. The 18th-century Gothic tower is by the celebrated John Carr, who was born at Horbury, near Wakefield. The Revd Patrick Brontë, father of the precociously gifted sisters, was briefly incumbent here.

There is no doubt, though, that Dewsbury was an important community even before the Conquest, as the church holds a range of worthy **Anglo-Saxon cross fragments**, together with a 'hog's-back' stone believed to be of English design (rather than Danish) and to date from the 800s. These are now well displayed in a special heritage centre.

A glance at the tower reminds us that here resides **'Black Tom'**, a bell legend says was given to the church in the 15th century by Thomas de Soothill after he killed his servant. Each Christmas Eve the bell tolls once for every year since Christ's birth, a ritual known as the 'Devil's Knell', in atonement for the crime.

Much of the glass in English churches is relatively new – with much redesign and restoration work having been done by the Victorians – but every so often a real gem of medieval date can be found. Here at All Saints it comes in the shape of three small agricultural scenes in the north transept window showing harvesting, threshing and pig-killing. Incredibly, they date from the 1200s.

Worth hunting for in the churchyard is the grave of Hannah Scott: the stone says she died in 1812 at the ripe old age of 804! Three years earlier, Patrick Brontë began his two-year curacy at the church and there is a memorial to him.

Dewsbury Museum is housed in a former textile magnate's mansion in what is now **Crow Nest Park**. It is on the Heckmondwike road and of particular interest to younger visitors. Here they can learn about childhood in days gone by, including how youngsters had to work in fields, factories and mines, and the strict manner in which they were educated.

EAST ARDSLEY [Leeds]

SE2925: 4 miles (6km) NW of Wakefield

This small town stands beside the busy M1. Its **reservoir**, built in the 19th century, is now more often than not covered by small boats and wildfowl, which find the water a useful stopping off point on their migration route. Much of its industry has gone, but a lot of hard work has gone into healing the scars of industrial processes to create new woodland areas and pleasant footpath routes.

Before the Victorian era the place

was little more than a small village, but the discovery of both iron and coal deposits in the vicinity led first to bell pits and later full-scale deep mining. Another 'industry', and one that still prospers, was the growing of rhubarb in long, dark forcing sheds. The railway that took the rhubarb, coal and iron products away was first opened as a horse-powered track in 1799. In 1857 the settlement was linked to the national rail network. **East Ardsley Station** once had two main lines passing through it and the nearby rail depot employed 400 men. The line has now gone, but the trackbeds provide a pleasant walking trail.

East Ardsley Colliery was opened in 1872, and as late as the 1960s pit ponies helped men haul the black gold from deep in the bowels of the earth. The pit has long since closed, but a local history trail passes a plaque marking the site on Moor Knoll Lane. Not far away, on Main Street, is **Perseverance Mill**, a characteristic red-brick building which produces rope and twine. Across the town is **Amblers Mill**, built just before the outbreak of the Great War and still producing the finest worsted cloth. Worsted is the finest woollen cloth, made from the best quality yarn and finely combed and closely twisted. It was (and remains in one or two places) the trademark of the West Riding, with Bradford known as the worsted capital of the world – the 'Worstedopolis'. The name comes from the village of Worstead near Norwich, the area that pio-

neered and dominated English woollen production in the early and Middle Ages.

The colliery has gone from East Ardsley and so has the town's famous ironworks, which closed during the depression of the 1930s and never reopened. In 1908 a blast furnace exploded, killing five workers and injuring another 13.

The **church of St Michael** was rebuilt in 1881, but worth a look is the south doorway, which was preserved from the earlier Norman building. It comes complete with characteristic zigzag carving and the almost pagan 'beak-heads'. These latter are an interesting reminder that the conversion to Christianity was never a simple process. Missionaries were always keen to set up their churches on the site of pre-Christian worship and often adopted both pagan feast days and the motifs and symbols of the earlier gods in order to attract their adherents. Beak-head carvings and the like helped ease the transition and are always worth looking out for while touring religious sites.

One of East Ardsley's best-known sons was the strange, 17th-century Quaker James Nayler. A man of eccentric, if not maniacal behaviour, he served in the parliamentary army during the Civil War and later became a follower of the then novel Quaker sect. His preaching was of the fire and brimstone variety, and he soon quarrelled with leading Quakers and toured the country with his own band of followers.

In 1656, he and his adherents rode into Bristol, with Nayler claiming to be the reincarnation of Christ. Not surprisingly for those intolerant times, he was arrested and charged with blasphemy. His punishment was to be pilloried and flogged in London. Not satisfied with that, the authorities bored a hole in his tongue and branded him on the forehead. The poor man was then thrown into gaol for two years. In 1660 he was set upon by highwaymen who robbed him and beat him so badly he later died.

EAST BRIERLEY [Kirklees]

SE1929: 3 miles (5km) SE of Bradford

This hilltop village is a pleasant place with, unusually for this part of Yorkshire, a village green with its own stocks and a lovely array of flowers in the spring. By the pond are **two stones**, known locally as the **'cup and saucer'**. Historians believe they were the site of an Anglo-Saxon cross and probably a meeting and worshipping point; one story says the cross was placed there by a Norman lord whose horse had killed a peasant.

EAST HARDWICK [Wakefield]

SE4618: 2 miles (3km) SE of Pontefract

The area around Pontefract is still pleasantly rural and this small village is a true farming community. People who commute to work occupy other homes, but the whole has a welcoming feel and some good footpaths to attract the walker. Historic buildings include some cottages of the early 18th century, but the **church of St Michael** was built in the last quarter of the 19th century.

EAST KESWICK [Leeds]

SE3644: 2 miles (4km) E of Harewood

Although ancient, and with a settlement dating back at least as early as the 900s, this village has in recent centuries been inextricably linked to the neighbouring great mansion and estate of Harewood House. Until the 1950s, when it had to be sold for death duties, much of the land round about was owned by the Lascelles family from the great house. The main local industry, apart from agriculture, which still flourishes, was the extraction of limestone for both building and for top dressing to improve arable land. The **church of St Mary Magdalen** was built in 1856.

ECCLESHILL [Bradford]

SE1734: 2 miles (4km) NE of Bradford

This small town's **church of St Luke** was built in 1848 and is a well proportioned example of workaday religious architecture of the period. A former woollen town, its most famous son is the artist David Hockney who was born here in 1937. Raised in the village, he studied at nearby Bradford College of Art and then the Royal College and was considered a major figure in the so-called 'Pop Art' movement of the late 1950s and 1960s. He is perhaps most famous for his 'swimming pool' pictures, inspired by the vivid colours and clean air of California which has long been his home. In recent years he has done much to merge the boundaries between painting and photography, with his Polaroid collage work receiving great critical acclaim. There is a changing exhibition of Hockney's vibrant and provocative work at **Saltaire**. Despite her son's fame and wealth, his mother has continued to live in Eccleshill.

Also here is **Bradford Industrial Museum,** which is based in the four-storey **Moorside Woollen Mill**. Naturally enough, the exhibits take the visitor through the history of Bradford's textile heritage with lots of machinery, looms and other manufacturing equipment. Of particular interest to younger visitors is a section devoted to the history of 'horses at work' which includes both static displays, and a chance to ride a horse-drawn tram.

ECCUP [Leeds]

SE2840: 5 miles (8km) SE of Otley

Not far from **Harewood House** and once part of the manor of nearby Arthington, tiny Eccup was called 'Echope' in the Domesday Book, a word from the Viking founders of the settlement meaning 'a gathering of high oak trees'. Now little more than a dormitory settlement, it stands beside the picturesque **Eccup Reservoir**, around whose shores there are pleasant walks.

ELLAND [Calderdale]

SE1021: 2½ miles (4km) SSE of Halifax

The motorist leaving the M62 and heading along the A629 to Halifax has a wonderful view of Elland, down in the valley to the left. It is the kind of view that should cause the visitor to exit this busy dual carriageway and take a look around a town which sits cosily in this sheltered bend in the River Calder. The name comes from 'ea-land', which means 'land close to water'.

The **church of St Mary** makes it clear that man has had a substantial presence here since the time of the Conquest. Although the building is largely 14th-century Perpendicular, there are remnants from a Norman church of around 1150 built in the structure. The pride of the building is its stained glass which, although much restored and replaced, dates back to 1481 and illustrates the life of the Virgin in no fewer than 21 scenes. There is also some good early work by Victorian glass artist C.E. Kempe.

Water has always been Elland's fortune, first via the river and the land it irrigated, and then thanks to the **Calder and Hebble Navigation** which went through the settlement in the early 19th century. One of Elland's best-known products was its durable flagstones that were quarried extensively in the area. They paved Halifax, Sowerby

Bridge and many other northern industrial towns, and while some are still to be admired the others only disappeared when 'progress' replaced them with tarmacadam. Had it not been for the canal, these extremely weighty consignments could not have been distributed.

As well as its woollen manufacture, Elland achieved fame in the 1960s as the home of the **Gannex** raincoat – the grand mill which bears their name can still be seen in the valley – which became a trademark of Labour Prime Minister Harold Wilson. Wilson hailed from over the hill in Huddersfield. Another industry particular to Elland is the production of 'boiled sweets' by the family firm of Dobsons. They have been making sweets in their factory on Northgate since 1850, and the principles of the task haven't changed much since. The works are open to visitors, but only as organised groups and by prior arrangement.

EMLEY [Wakefield]

SE2413: 6 miles (10km) ESE of Huddersfield

You might never have been to Emley, but there is every chance that if you have ever ventured within 20 miles of it on a clear day you have seen its mast. **Emley Moor television mast** reaches 900ft (300m) into the air, with another 180ft of aerial on top. Add that height to a substantial elevation above sea level and you have a landmark of gigantic proportions. The great concrete structure, which transmits signals to five million homes, is taller than the Eiffel Tower and replaced an earlier, shorter mast which collapsed

Market Cross, Emley

during a storm in 1969 (the photographs of the event and its aftermath are remarkable).

If the mast is one reason to visit this windswept Pennine market village, then its history is another. Over the centuries it has balanced industry in the form of ironstone mining, with providing grazing for sheep; together they have created a compact centre with plenty of reminders of earlier times. The middle of Emley, the site of a weekly market chartered in 1253 by Henry III, still has the **market cross**. Unfortunately, it is now little more than a stump and, painted white and often surrounded by bedding plants, acts as a kind of impromptu traffic island. It has seen some sights but none odder than that in 1826, when John Turton sold his wife Mary for two half-crowns (25pence) to William Kaye of Scissett. Remarkably, when Kaye popped his clogs, Mary came home and lived with her romantic husband for another 30 years; whether she brought the 'five bob' with her is unknown.

What the village elders thought of this incident is unclear, but the **church of St Michael** stands nearby. It is an ancient building with a Norman nave, and a tympanum of the same period built into the later Perpendicular south wall; look out for the faded carving of the dragon and the lamb. The impressive tower is also of the 15th century, while there is some rare medieval stained glass, including a scene of the crucifixion with characterisations of the Virgin and St John. There is an 18th-century pulpit, complete with sounding board to keep dozy members of the congregation awake, and some old box pews. There are a number of interesting bits of masonry built into the churchyard wall, including what some consider might be the remains of a stone cross from the Hospitaler knights who owned property in the area in the Middle Ages. There is also a stone from above the doorway of the now demolished **Wrigglesworth School** which edifyingly reads:

'If fortune keep thee warm
Thy friends around thee swarm
Like bees around a honey pot
But if she frowns and casts thee (off)
Lye there and rott.'

The prosperity of Emley came in the 12th century in the shape of ironstone mining by monks who established a 'grange' here. Cistercians from Byland Abbey established themselves in the vicinity in 1171, at a site about a mile from the centre of Emley known ever since as **Bentley Grange**. Here they dug into the ground and, as they encountered the valuable ironstone widened out the excavation underground, creating 'bell pits', so-called because of their shape. The excavated rubbish was thrown onto the surface and can still be seen in these fields to this day, especially from the air. Once they had removed the iron-rich ore it would be smelted nearby in furnaces heated by locally produced charcoal and worked by machinery powered by a nearby stream.

ESHOLT [Bradford]

SE1841: 2 miles (3km) SW of Guiseley

This hamlet in a wooded and green valley seems a world away from the bustling towns of Guiseley, Baildon and Garforth nearby. In ancient times it was the site of a priory founded in the 12th century, the site of which is now occupied by **Esholt Hall**. Some of the old priory is contained in this grand Queen Anne-style house. Completed in 1709, it now houses offices and conference facilities for Yorkshire Water and is not open to the public.

The village proper is also interesting, notably as the setting for the Dales village of 'Emmerdale' in the Yorkshire Television soap of the same name. Wander around and see where Seth tramps with his dog and where Alan Turner serves best bitter in the Woolpack. The pub – whose frontage appears in the series but whose interior is entirely different – was recently renamed to take that given it in the programme.

Nearby, on Chapel Lane, the visitor with children in tow will enjoy **St Leonard's Heritage Farm Park**. This is not a museum but a working, family-run dairy farm that keeps a range of rare breeds and other domestic animals. Milking takes place daily and townies can watch the process in detail. There is also a café.

FAIRBURN INGS [Leeds]

SE4527: 1 mile (2km) N of Castleford

The small sandstone-coloured village of Fairburn is pleasant enough, but it is the huge expanse of flooded land and low pasture below it which attracts the visitor. Visible from the A1, and easily reached from this road, the **Fairburn Ings Nature Reserve** is one of the most important sites in the region for migrating and breeding birds. Managed by the Royal Society for the Protection of Birds, the reserve came into being in 1968 and now employs a full-time warden, other staff and has a visitor centre and a number of observation hides and walking trails.

Close to the River Aire, it was once flooded regularly by this waterway. The word 'ing' is common enough in these parts and has its origins in Old Norse. It means 'damp or marshy land'. A flood bank built in the 18th century helped the land dry out and it was then used as pastureland. Over the last century, mining beneath the site caused subsidence, which in turn has produced huge expanses of permanent standing water. Colliery spoil heaps have been overgrown with woodland and the end result is an excellent location for both dedicated birdwatchers and those keen to learn more about the hobby.

In winter, large numbers of wildfowl find refuge here from the cold of their Scandinavian breeding grounds, while important numbers of gulls roost at Fairburn in the evenings. In spring and autumn, waders and other passage migrants call in; while during the summer swans, waterfowl and large numbers of waders breed on the reserve.

FARNLEY [Leeds]

SE2532: 3 miles (5km) SE of Leeds

There's an Old Farnley and a New Farnley, but it has to be the latter which attracts attention, for there stands **Farnley Hall.** This was proclaimed by rigorously demanding architectural historian Nikolaus Pevsner as 'perhaps John Carr's masterpiece'. The Yorkshire genius – designer of Harewood House – built this home in the late 1780s, at the height of his powers, and he managed to tack a Georgian building onto a substantial and attractive Elizabethan mansion without spoiling either.

John Ruskin, the great Victorian artist and moral philosopher, fell in love with the place because of the then wondrous collection of paintings by J.M.W. Turner at the hall. Turner, the inspiration of a million reproductions, was a friend of Thomas Fawkes, who owned the property, and a regular visitor over many years beginning in 1797. The squire was in no doubt about Turner's talents and bought an estimated 200 pictures and drawings from him for a total of £3000 – a huge sum at today's values.

Unfortunately, the house is not open to the public, but the grounds are and are a pleasant area for a Sunday afternoon 'breather'.

FARNLEY TYAS [Kirklees]

SE1612: 2 miles (4km) SE of Huddersfield

This village stands in a rural location and was once dominated by agriculture. Now it is popular with commuters who work elsewhere and crave its peace. In between, in the 18th century in particular, it housed a whole range of cloth tradespeople working from their own homes or small workshops.

The suffix 'Tyas' dates from the 1200s when the Le Tyeis family owned the manor, but it was the Kaye-Dartmouths who built **Woodsome Hall** in the 16th century. The building is, in fact, classified as standing in the neighbouring hamlet of **Fenay Bridge** and now serves as a golf club. Its symmetrical front provides a classic Elizabethan view and the main hall originally had an open roof: a gem.

The **church of St Lucius** was built in 1840, evidence that at the time the village had a considerable and growing population.

FARSLEY [Leeds]

SE2135: 1 mile (2km) NW of Pudsey

Always a place where wool has been worked, Farsley's fortunes were transformed at the beginning of the 19th century. Until that time the traditional cottage industry of cloth production had provided clothing and a little extra for the local inhabitants, while one or two more enterprising souls did a little better. One such family was the Gaunts, who can trace their involvement in woollen manufacture in Farsley back to Elizabethan times (they are still here, still running the family firm and producing fine worsteds).

But it was Samuel Marsden, 'the flogging parson', who altered life in Farsley forever. Born in the village in 1764, he arrived in New South Wales as a clergyman three decades later and farmed at Parramatta. Appointed a magistrate, he was so fierce in his suppression of a rising by Irish convicts that he earned the aforementioned title. Despite his strict views on law and order, he was liberal and inventive in his agrarian pursuits, and excelled at breeding sheep for wool production. In 1807 he brought the first commercial assignment of Australian wool to England, and his hometown.

Not satisfied with transforming a whole economy – or perhaps two if you count that of Australia – he also travelled to New Zealand and conducted the first Christian service there in 1814.

Inevitably, Farsley boasts the **Samuel Marsden Memorial Gardens**, an obelisk in the churchyard and a window in the **church of St John.**

FEATHERSTONE [Wakefield]

SE4222: 2½ miles (4km) SW of Pontefract

This proud, no-nonsense West Yorkshire town has, very sadly, seen its heyday come and go. For a century its collieries provided work and a hard but honest livelihood for thousands of men and their families. The decline and effective destruction of the coal mining industry after the 1984-85 strike saw all Featherstone's pits close – and their miners thrown on the scrap heap. Attempts have been made to create new jobs and retrain the unemployed, but these are not problems that can easily be solved.

The **church of All Saints** is medieval in date with some remnants on display in the nave and chancel. Unfortunately, the obsession the Victorians had with 'improving' any church they could get their hands on means this one has been drastically altered to suit 19th-century taste – or lack of it.

It remains the home of the once great Featherstone Rovers Rugby League side. In keeping with others they have now changed their name – in this case to the Featherstone Lions.

FELKIRK [Wakefield]

SE3812: 7 miles (12km) SW of Pontefract

This small village is another in the West Yorkshire coalfield which over the past century has accrued a large number of new buildings, to the extent that its original character is hard to define. Unlike many others, however, it has one remarkable feature that makes a stop while in the area a 'must' for all those interested in church architecture.

St Peter's Church is largely Early English in character, with many features from that late 13th century period including octagonal piers and chamfered arches, and fine chancel chapels. Interestingly though, there are a number of Norman influences which have confused experts; it might even be that the Norman church stood on a slightly different site and was moved and rebuilt in its present position within a century or two of its original construction. Whatever happened, there remains an ancient porch and doorway and carved stones in the tower dating back to the time of the Conqueror. Unusual and very rare is an inlaid bench dating to the 16th century.

From the same period, close by the church is a plain but important **Elizabethan schoolhouse,** reminding us of the ancient links between organised learning and religion.

FERRYBRIDGE [Wakefield]

SE4824: 2 miles (3km) E of Castleford

The most many of us see of Ferrybridge is a fleeting glimpse as we dash by on the busy A1. Before the last war, travellers went straight through the village on the route of what was then the Great North Road. As a result, historians tell us, Cardinal Wolsey confirmed 200 children on his way from his Archbishopric of York to London to answer charges of high treason. Perhaps fortunately for the once all-powerful prelate, he died before he arrived at the Tower and denied Henry VIII his head.

Always an important crossing point on the River Aire – hence the descriptive name – armies have come and gone this way from Roman legions to Yorkists and Lancastrians on their way to the carnage at nearby Towton in 1461.

Interestingly, and for some bizarre reason, the town's most important building, **the church of St Andrew,** was taken down, piece by piece, in 1952. Apparently to have it nearer the centre of the town close to the market place, workmen then proceeded to rebuild this largely 13th-century structure, only to ham-fistedly manage to place the south door on the north side and the north aisle on the south side! Apart from marvelling at this feat of 'cowboy' building, take a look at the unusual, reeded, bowl-shaped font. Its origins are uncertain, but could be Norman.

The marvellous 1797 **bridge** over the Aire by John Carr is bypassed by the A1. It stands in the shadow of Ferrybridge's main landmark, the huge **power station** complex that can be seen from 30 miles away on the southern fringes of South Yorkshire.

FITZWILLIAM [Wakefield]

SE4115: 5 miles (8km) SE of Wakefield

Until the 1970s there were half a dozen coal mines within walking distance of this small and dour-looking village. Its name comes from the vastly wealthy landowning family whose fortunes originally came from agriculture but who also prospered from coal. The Fitzwilliams held lands across the country and were never resident in this area.

The village's claim to fame is that in the 1940s one youngster playing cricket in the alleys between its regimented rows of pit houses grew up to be one of Yorkshire and England's finest batsmen. Geoffrey Boycott was born here in 1940 and was capped by his county 23 years later. He played 108 times for England and scored more than 150 centuries; arguably his finest was his 'hundredth hundred' against Australia, appropriately enough at **Headingley**, in 1977.

FLANSHAW [Wakefield]

SE3121: 2 miles (3km) W of Wakefield

This small hamlet was once an agricultural area, but in more recent times industries including the manufacture of cocoa matting and sweet-making provided employment. This latter, thanks to the firm Talbot's, made, amongst other things, Yorkshire Mixture: boiled sweets in various shapes and flavours sold by weight in paper bags. The firm has gone – and so have the paper bags, to be replaced by anonymous confections sold sanitised and characterless in plastic shrink-wrapping; the price we pay for progress.

FRICKLEY [Wakefield]

SE4609: 2 miles (3km) S of South Elmsall

It is hard to say quite what Frickley is. If it is a village in the real sense, where does it begin and nearby South Elmsall end – or indeed Clayton in the opposite direction? A few houses by the road may make up the village, but something more substantial must have occu-

pied the site centuries ago – otherwise why build the lovely, yet isolated and lonely-looking **church of All Saints**? In Victorian times, during the great dash for coal, **Frickley Colliery** was sunk and provided work for men and boys from the villages around the area, but now it has closed. Happily, the brass band that takes its name survives, as does the soccer team, also named after this enigmatic 'village'.

The church is certainly worth a visit. It stands in a field and has a Norman chancel arch and a host of other features which date the bulk of the building to the late 13th and early 14th centuries. Of particular note are the gilded pulpit and organ case.

FULNECK [Leeds]

SE2132: 4 miles (6km) E of Bradford

There are some who might argue this 'settlement' should be classed as part of Pudsey; after all, one runs into the other. But the history of Fulneck is so unlike that of any other town in the county, or perhaps even the country, that it deserves a place of its own.

Fulneck was settled in 1742 by the brethren of the **Moravian Church**, a non-conformist group from Bohemia led by a Count Von Zinzendorf, whose simplistic and peaceful views on life greatly influenced John Wesley. Why they settled here is unknown, but in doing so they constructed a collection of buildings worthy of a visit. It included houses for single men and for single women, a chapel, a school, a house for widows and a family house. There was also a schoolhouse, in which lived boys and girls who were either orphaned or whose parents were working abroad as missionaries. As the community grew in the 1700s, the buildings created the longest Georgian terrace in Europe.

Happily, this fascinating heritage has been preserved and a small **museum** is housed in a pair of original cottages, recreating life in the community in the last century. It looks at the Moravian Church in an international context, and at the local situation. In addition, the museum contains a Victorian parlour, Moravian embroidery, the village fire engine from the time of George IV and an operational loom.

The **church** was built between 1746-8 with a classical interior and galleries on three sides. The organ is of the same period and a rare example of its kind.

GARFORTH [Leeds]

SE4133: 6 miles (10km) W of Leeds

A workaday town, Garforth's main public building of interest is the early Victorian **church of St Mary**, built in 1844. Complete with spire-topped tower it is executed in the lancet style with tall, slim and pointed windows. Inside stands part of an **Anglo-Saxon cross** with interlacing.

GOLCAR [Kirklees]

SE0915: 3 miles (5km) WSW of Huddersfield

One author suggests Golcar resembles an Italian village because it sits on the side of a hill. The nearest thing to Italy found in Golcar is a packet of spaghetti bought from the local co-op – not that the Mediterranean country, nor this welcoming place, needs the other in any way. A traditional Pennine hill town, it has plenty of buildings from the Victorian era, plus more than a few from a century and more earlier when many families would have spun and woven local wool in their own homes. One such place, and the main reason for the visitor to come to Golcar, has been turned into the **Colne Valley Museum.**

In 1970 a voluntary trust took a terrace of three, three-storey weaver's cottages and turned them into a superb recreation of local industrial life in the 1850s. Like so many others, these cottages had a ground floor with a fireplace in the main living area and a second floor where the whole family would have slept. The third floor – illuminated by light from south-facing mullioned windows running the length of the building – was where the womenfolk would have spun thread from the fleeces and where the men and boys would have worked at the handloom. Here, typically, there is a 'tekkin' in door' at the rear of the building to allow easy access in and out for wool and the finished product. The museum curators have recreated a series of scenes including a weaver's living room complete with woollen rag rugs, an open range in the fireplace, a spare wooden table – the focal point of family life – and even a wooden 'rack' hanging from the ceiling where clothes would have been put to dry.

The next floor demonstrates the processes involved in preparing the wool, from preparing the fibres, or 'carding', by hand to spinning wheels of various designs and antiquity. The beauty of the museum is that there are always people using the machinery and demonstrating these age-old skills, making it an ideal attraction for youngsters.

On the top floor is the loom chamber, which includes an example of both a handloom and a Spinning Jenny. Weavers were always ahead of the production of yarn to work with; many spinners needed to keep busy to supply even the simplest of looms. In 1770 James Hargreaves solved the supply problem by inventing the 'Spinning Jenny', one of the first machines which led up to the mechanisation of the Industrial Revolution. Also on the top floor is a traditional **clogger's shop** of around 1910. The benches, gaslights and tools all came from the shop of Albert Parkin who worked in Carr Lane at nearby Slaithwaite. Craftsmen still work here on open days, demonstrating the old skills and selling the sturdy footwear which, a century ago, everybody in a town like Golcar wore. The **church of St John** was completed in 1830, one of the many 'Waterloo' churches thrown up by the Church of England in order to bring their message to burgeoning industrial settlements at a time when the Nonconformists were most active.

GOMERSAL [Kirklees]

SE2026: 4½ miles (7km) SSE of Bradford

An interesting town in the Spen Valley, Gomersal witnessed some of the rabble-rousing which soon developed into the Luddite risings of 1812 in opposition to the growing mechanisation of the textile industry. The unrest exploded into violence in nearby Huddersfield, with a number of rioters killed and more injured. Some ringleaders were executed at York. These tragic events provided material for Charlotte Brontë (who came here in the 1830s) and found voice in her novel *Shirley*. Charlotte knew Gomersal as the hometown of her friend Mary Taylor, who lived with her welcoming family at **Red House.**

Built in 1660, from brick rather than the traditional and more common local stone – hence its descriptive name – it is now a museum with free admission. The novelist ensured the house immortality by renaming it 'Briarmains' and describing its appearance and contents in detail. Seen today, Red House has been restored and set out as it would have been when Queen Victoria began her reign, with an elegant parlour and stone-flagged kitchen. The stained-glass windows described by Charlotte in detail are still there, together with permanent displays telling the story of the house and its famous visitor. The previous century another famous and regular visitor was the Methodist John Wesley who drew great crowds when he preached from a rear window. Also in Gomersal is the **'Pork Pie Chapel'**, a Methodist church dated 1827 and known for its semicircular frontage.

GOOSE EYE [Bradford]

SE0240: 2½ miles (4km) W of Keighley

This is a pleasant enough hamlet on the edge of Keighley which would not normally merit a place in a guide such as this. One very good reason, however, more than justifies its inclusion. The village pub is the centre of any community, and **The Turkey** at Goose Eye is justifiably famous. Tucked away down a walled lane at the bottom of a steep valley, this cosy and welcoming pub serves Goose Eye Bitter which is brewed nearby.

GREENGATES [Bradford]

SE1937: 4 miles (6km) NNE of Bradford

The **church of St John the Evangelist** was built in 1893 and, while pleasant enough, is not the real reason to come to this small village. Close by, at Apperley Bridge, is the **George and Dragon Inn,** which has stood here since the 16th century. The building is so important that it is one of the few pubs featured by the architectural historian Nikolaus Pevsner in his classic *Buildings of West Yorkshire*. The two-storey building has a gabled front and typical mullioned windows with ancient timber framing inside. A new wing was added in the reign of Queen Anne and on a lintel of a fireplace on the upper floor is carved the following, 'Not for the purpose of making a show but for necessary uses Samuel Hemingway and Mary his wife enlarged this house A.D. 1704. These things are cherishing: victuals, drink, warmth, shelter, which if thow possess, remember gratefully to give thanks to God.'

GREETLAND [Calderdale]

SE0921: 2½ miles (4km) S of Halifax

A surprising place this, in the heart of Calderdale and yet especially beautiful. Here, at **North Dean Woods** is the start of the Calderdale Way. Ask at the information centre here for details of several pleasant woodland walks of lesser distance. Nearby is **Clay House** in West Vale, an impressive yeoman farmer's house of the 1600s, complete with an unusual barn of a similar date. Historians believe a long-lost Roman town named in the chronicles as 'Cambodunum' could have been located in the area following the discovery of a Roman altar with the date AD205.

GUISELEY [Leeds]

SE1942: 2½ miles (4km) SW of Otley

For the last 70 years the town of Guiseley, or rather the small settlement of **White Cross** nearby, has been synonymous with that great social leveller – fish and chips. Harry Ramsden started selling his delicacy from a small shed next to the tram stop here in 1928. Three years later he built a restaurant that quickly doubled in size. By the 1960s **Harry Ramsden's** proudly claimed to be the 'biggest fish and chip shop in the world'. It might well still be, but now the boast is that it makes the best fish and chips on the planet. From humble beginnings the name has travelled the world with restaurants in Hong Kong and the Persian Gulf. The grand 1930s restaurant is still at White Cross and remains a place every visitor should try at least once.

One thousand years ago a settlement had already developed at Guiseley, attracted here by a series of pure, flowing **wells** which gave a number of local streets and features their names. By the time of the Conquest it was a fair-sized agricultural community, significant enough to justify the foundation of the **church of St Oswald.** Now it is of major significance for historians as it is complete with several Norman features including an impressive doorway, and many Early English characteristics including an excellent south transept and chancel arch. The church was the one used by generations of the Longfellow family. The grandfather of the famous American poet left here to seek his fortune in the New World in the 18th century. Married here in 1812 were Patrick Brontë and Maria Branwell. The young curate then stood at the altar and performed the wedding ceremony for his friend, the vicar who had just conducted the Brontë's nuptials.

Nearby is a splendid Elizabethan **rectory** built in 1601 around a medieval hall.

HALIFAX [Calderdale]

SE0925: 7 miles (11km) NNW of Huddersfield

Although all of them existed prior to the industrialisation which overtook the north of England in the final quarter of the 18th century, Leeds, Bradford and Halifax were all market towns of much smaller size than they later became. The latter, however, was the largest of them all, and of the three retains the most from its pre-Industrial Revolution past. While most towns and villages in the West Riding had their 'domestic system' of woollen cloth production, involving families working together in their own homes, only a few became known as centres for that trade. After all, once made, these bolts of cloth, or 'pieces' had to be sold on before they could be turned into garments and other items.

The position of Halifax, in this trading hierarchy is hard to imagine now, when set against its much larger neighbours, but a glance at the town's parish church gives the game away. It was a manufacturing centre, one on which textile trading was based, and a base for clothing manufacturers; together they created an industrial town at least 300 years before many others in the county. The **parish church of St John** is one of the largest and most impressive in the country. All the evidence points to the fact that success in commerce in medieval times was almost always expressed in architecture, often in domestic buildings, but regularly in ecclesiastical ones. In an age when man felt very close to his god at all times, rich men spent their money on their local church; and this one is a perfect example of that spiritual devotion. It dates back at least to the 12th century, but what we see today in this cathedral-like structure is more typical of the Perpendicular style of the 15th century. The most impressive feature, and the one which ensures the church remains a landmark despite the mills which come to the very centre of the town even today, is the west tower which was completed in 1480. It comes with all the usual adornments, battlements, pinnacles and classical angled buttresses. Inside, all is grand and airy and the visitor should stop to admire the finely wrought wooden ceilings in nave and chancel and dated to 1636.

The **windows** are large and show off the glass, some of which is credited to the period of Cromwell's time as Protector and therefore rare, to its best effect. Other items of note inside the church include an elaborately carved wooden font cover from the 1400s, a beautifully carved communion rail and some plain 17th-century box pews. **Monuments** are largely Georgian and commemorate local philanthropists and others whose wealth was made from the town's important economic position. The most remarkable item in the church, though, must be the life-size wooden figure of **Old Tristram**. This ingenious, and extremely rare, form of poor box bears the date 1701, but his clothing, of long coat, stockings and buckled shoes suggests he could be half a century older. His long, flowing beard and balding head are so realistic that some have claimed he represents a real person, perhaps a beggar who regularly asked for alms at the church door, or while wandering through the streets of the town. Poor boxes were – and in some cases remain – familiar items in churches, and Old Tristram's box is surmounted by the plea: 'Pray Remember The Poor'.

If Halifax was important in the 15th century, it was more so in the 18th. By this time, rich merchants and clothiers had the system of textile manufacture and trade well in hand. Halifax and the surrounding area was a particularly important centre for fine worsteds, and it was to the town that the cloth was brought for sale. Other towns also had their cloth halls where the trading was done, but Halifax had the finest. Luckily for all of us, the **Halifax Piece Hall** survives to this day and is still a hive of activity. In its heyday, it was opened on January 1, 1779, it was a bustling centre containing 315 merchant's trading rooms set around a broad square. A grade one listed building today, it has an Italianate flavour to the design, comprising two-storey colonnaded galleries all round, complete with pillars and archways. The large cobbled square in the middle would be used by less well-off traders who would rent the space by the day, while the grassed areas were available for grazing sheep. Interestingly, when first opened the Piece Hall was only open for business for two hours on Saturday mornings.

Despite the obvious wealth of its builders, the cottage industry the Piece Hall represents was already on its way out. Mechanisation meant that within a couple of decades textile barons with their own huge factories no longer needed to deal in such a 'piecemeal' way and by-passed this form of commerce. The Piece Hall, however, continued in use as a public market after 1871. These days it contains numerous antique shops, booksellers and food stalls, while the central square is covered in colourful stalls and the site of public entertainment every weekend. No visit to Halifax is complete without an hour or two in the Piece Hall.

The site also includes the entrance to the **Calderdale Industrial Museum**, via the Piece Hall Art Gallery – a space for contemporary exhibitions. The museum tells the story of Calderdale's industrial and pre-industrial past through the eyes of ordinary people and their hard and dreary lives in the mills. Exhibits include examples of the machinery used in both the familiar weaver's cottages, and their colossal successors which transformed Yorkshire into one of the world's great manufacturing

powerhouses. There is a Spinning Jenny, a Flying Shuttle and a restored beam engine. The first section covers the period between 1450 and 1830 – before the major factories were built – and then moves into a period when engineering, carpet manufacture and other industries joined woollen manufacture in the town. Recreations of coal and brick-clay mines, made more authentic with sound and smells, make it even more interesting, especially for children.

Unlike some of its neighbours, Halifax still retains many of the buildings constructed during the frenetic days of Victorian expansion and is considered by many as one of the finest examples of an industrial town of the late 19th century. Grand houses, self-important office blocks, Nonconformist chapels and the mills where the 'brass' was made can all be found here in large numbers; there are still, thankfully, a few factory chimneys left too. One of the most interesting mill complexes is the **Dean Clough Mills** project on the edge of the town centre beside the A629 Keighley road.

Once a massive carpet mill – said to have been the biggest in the world – employing more than 4000 men and women, its success and its jobs ebbed away after the Second World War. On the verge of dereliction, it captured the imagination of energetic entrepreneur Sir Ernest Hall who rescued it and has effected a transformation. The buildings now house design companies, media businesses, IT specialists and even include some excellent gallery and exhibition space. Included among the galleries is the **Henry Moore Studio**, a workplace for contemporary artists to create and display their skills.

As for chimneys, the Halifax skyline is graced with one of the most remarkable in the country – not that it ever conveyed smoke skyward. **Wainhouse's Tower**, on the A646 south-west of the town centre, reaches 275ft into the air and was built in the 1870s. J.E. Wainhouse was a successful businessman with a love of buildings and constructed the chimney beside his dye works. The idea was that the structure would have a spiral staircase around the outside, and it was then cased in stone. The whole thing is covered in ornamentation and Wainhouse used to climb its 400 steps to enjoy the view from the top; his plans for an observatory there were foiled when it was discovered that his cupola provided insufficient room to manoeuvre a telescope!

One of Halifax's most intriguing sites, and one loved by ghoulish youngsters, is the town **gibbet**. Reputed to have been the scene of 80 public executions until the practice was abandoned in 1650, a replica of this pre-French Revolution guillotine stands, not surprisingly, in Gibbet Street. The merchant clothiers, so jealous of their rights and privileges, made it a capital offence to steal a piece of cloth worth more than 13 old pence, on pain of beheading. The gibbet was infa-

mous across the region and gave rise to the once familiar cry, 'From Hell, Hull and Halifax, Good Lord Deliver Us!' Why Hull was included in the trinity is unclear. The original axe head that provided the cutting edge for this barbarous tool of public order is retained at **Bankfield Museum.**

The museum stands in **Ackroyd Park**, just a mile north of the town on the A647. From 1857, Bankfield was the home of Edward Ackroyd, the biggest wool manufacturer in the country. A man of immense wealth, he was responsible for the neighbouring model mill village of **Ackroyden** – a concept copied a short time later by Sir Titus Salt at **Saltaire** near Bradford. The village came complete with allotments, a public park, co-operative store and, of course, its own church. His mansion is of Italian style with masses of marble; ornate painted ceilings and lavish interiors. It has been a museum since 1887 and houses an internationally important collection of textiles and costumes from around the world. Garments as diverse as wrappings from Egyptian mummies, from Africa, India and the Far East make up the 'World of Textiles' exhibition. Space is also devoted to the exploration of textile collector Edith Durham who travelled to the Balkans and Russia at the turn of the 20th century and returned with a collection of world importance. Bankfield is also the official museum of the Duke of Wellington's Regiment and items on display include the original wellington boots. A proud regiment which recruits across the former West Riding, it dates back to 1702 and has a brave and illustrious history.

Another major public building that deserves a look as you wander around is the **town hall** on Broad Street. This is a classic of Victorian design, executed by Sir Charles Barry between 1859 and 1862 and completed by his son Edward Middleton Barry. Sir Charles was a major figure in his period, being responsible for, amongst many other great buildings, the new Palace of Westminster in 1840. That Halifax could afford such a remarkable architect – similar to a provincial town these days attracting Sir Richard Rogers to take on a commission – is evidence of both the depth of Halifax's pockets and the pride of its leading citizens. Many northern industrial towns are graced by such grandiose town halls, including Leeds, Bradford, Sheffield, Bolton and Rochdale.

If these great towns and cities had their town halls, they more often than not also had their grand public markets. Industrialisation and massive expansion of the townscape often meant the tradition marketplace in the medieval town centre was brushed away. The competition to build impressive replacements was fierce – the town of Halifax had three markets, including the Piece Hall. The impressive **Borough Market** on Princess Street was opened in 1896 by the Duke of York (later George V). The building is made – inevitably considering the period – from

wrought and cast iron, creating an airy, soaring roof structure with a mosque-like brightly pained interior. The local architects were also responsible for **Leeds City Markets** opened a few years later.

For children, Halifax has one of the most interesting attractions in the region. **Eureka!** is dubbed a 'museum for children', but forget the images which come to mind of dusty glass cases and meaningless exhibits – this is a fun and learning factory of the first rank. Designed for children aged from three to 12 years of age, there are hands-on displays covering everything from the human body to what makes a toilet flush, from how television programmes are made to how we live and work together. Eureka! has its own shop and café, but there are facilities for picnics. It can be found close to the restored railway station on Horton Street.

Another attraction for children is **Horses at Work – The National Museum of the Working Horse** in – appropriately enough – Dobbin's Yard off South Parade. Here visitors, and it is particularly appealing to children, can see demonstrations of grooming and harnessing, and horses working with the vehicles which before the advent of the motor car were a familiar sight in our towns and cities.

HARDEN [Bradford]

SE0838: 2 miles (4km) W of Bingley

This small village is full of history,

there having been a settlement on the site since Anglo-Saxon times when it was known as 'Hateltone'. Nearby **Harden Moor** is the location of two Bronze Age **burial mounds** and a stone circle from the same period. It is easy to see why folk were attracted to this sheltered location. For much of the Middle Ages the land was farmed and mined (for ironstone) by the Cistercian monks from Rievaulx Abbey. To the south-east of the village is a feature known as **Fairfax's Intrenchement**, an earthwork bank said to have been part of the Civil War defensive structure. The great Parliamentary general is reputed to have stayed at **Harden Grange**, home of the local landowners, the Ferrands. Sir Thomas Fairfax, himself a West Yorkshireman, from Denton, in Wharfedale, was the victor at Naseby and his family were once major landowners throughout the West Riding.

Just north of Harden Grange is **St Ives**, another home of the Ferrands, this time dating from the 19th century. Here the Prime Minister Benjamin Disraeli was a regular visitor and is believed to have used scenes in the area for his well-known Chartist novel *Sybil*. Above the village of Harden is a classic of Victorian 'folly' architecture. **St David's Ruin** was built in 1796, again by one of the Ferrand dynasty, and could be seen from Harden Grange across the valley. The tower comprises a cylindrical structure of one (and a half) storeys, with pointed arches to the door and windows – another pointed arch stands nearby.

HAREWOOD [Leeds]

SE3145: 6 miles (10km) S of Harrogate

What a fascinating ensemble this is, comprising a model village, ancient castle, attractive church and the great house on which all depended. Taking the last first, **Harewood House** was begun in 1759 for the wealthy Lascelles family who had bought the estate after making a fortune in haberdashery and customs work in the West Indies. The architects of the grand design were John Carr of York, who married one of the Lascelles daughters, and who was just 36 when this masterpiece was erected, and the even younger Robert Adam.

The building is huge, sitting amidst vast parkland, and comes complete with all the columns, high windows and other grand effects from what was, arguably, the best period in English classical architecture. Inside, the visitor can enjoy fine Adam touches, such as the Doric-columned entrance hall and the music room with wall panels by Zucchi and Angelica Kauffmann. Everywhere there is furniture by the great Otley craftsman Thomas Chippendale, while the dining hall, although altered in the middle of the 19th century by Sir Thomas Barry (he also greatly altered the southern facade in the 1840s), is splendid and still used for grand occasions. The current Lord Harewood, a cousin of the Queen, still lives at Harewood House and the excellent state of repair of the building is credit to his devotion. Capability Brown designed the grounds. His appellation came not from his aversion to his Christian name, Lancelot, but from his assertion when meeting a rich client that their grounds had excellent 'capabilities'.

Standing alone in the parkland of the great house is the **church of All Saints.** Built in the Perpendicular style, and dating to the 15th century, it is lonely now only because the Lascelles decided to move the ancient village of Harewood outside the walls of the park and thus, conveniently, out of their sensitive sight. A pleasant enough building, its great attraction is its unique collection of six medieval funerary monuments spanning the 100 years beginning in 1419. All but one is alabaster, with three in the south aisle and chapel being dedicated to the Gascoigne family who lived at the now ruined Gawthorpe House nearby. All the men appear in armour, except one who wears judge's robes. He was a Lord Chief Justice and died in 1419. He appears in Shakespeare's *Henry IV* when he takes the youthful future King Henry V to court for adolescent misdemeanours. Other grand tombs, with knights in armour and women in widow's weeds, commemorate other great families with links to Harewood. Together they provide an interesting lesson in Tudor fashions and customs. Sir George Gilbert Scott altered the interior of the church considerably in the Victorian era – a common act of vandalism at that time.

The aforementioned village of Harewood now stands outside the main entrance to Harewood House on the former turnpike road from Leeds to Harrogate. Once again, John Carr was the architect of these terraced buildings in the same warm orange sandstone as the main house.

Not far away, but sadly not open to the general public, is **Harewood Castle,** dated to 1367 and home to the Alburghs. Although ruined, the remaining walls are more than 2 metres (7ft) thick in some places with standing towers and a main entrance complete with evidence of the former portcullis. The great hall is visible and has a large fireplace with a solar above connecting with a chapel.

HARTSHEAD [Kirklees]

SE1723: 4½ miles (7km) W of Dewsbury

That this village existed in pre-Conquest times is clear from the **Walton Cross** that stands about a quarter of a mile from the village church. The cross, although difficult to date precisely, is of Viking origin and maybe as old at the 8th century. Inevitably, it is well worn, but we can still make out two mythical beasts facing each other, plenty of clever scrolling, and four birds – use your imagination and they can be sitting in a tree.

Inside the **church of St Peter** the font base is Anglo-Saxon and the south doorway is Norman, complete with the diagnostic zigzag pattern in the arch. The short tower is also of the 12th century, but the rest of the church is dated 1881. Those responsible for the rebuilding echoed the Norman style perfectly, but the new work means some of the atmosphere has gone. While he would recognise the door, the Revd Patrick Brontë, the young curate who came here in 1811, would struggle to acknowledge the rest. This Irish clergyman spent four years in what was soon to become a busy woollen and manufacturing town, and here met his future wife, the long-suffering Maria Branwell who hailed from Cornwall. They were married at Guiseley in 1812. Their first child, also Maria, was born here in 1814, and her sister Elizabeth a year later. Both died young. The three great literary sisters were born when the couple moved from Hartshead, first to Thornton and then to Haworth – as was their wayward brother Branwell.

The old **parish school** stands in the churchyard. Not far away from Hartshead was **Kirklees Hall**, one of the sites in the north country associated with the legendary Robin Hood and one of the places which can claim to hold his grave.

HARTSHEAD MOOR [Kirklees]

SE1624: 2 miles (3kn) NNE of Brighouse

Perched on the edge of the Pennine Moors, this is little more than a small hamlet, but one which in the West Yorkshire tradition once boasted its own institute for the improvement of worker's minds and a Methodist chapel. In the 19th century, mining was an important industry, but these days it is more a dormitory settlement for people working in the major towns and stands not far from the M62 trans-Pennine motorway. Back in 1974 the **Hartshead Moor service station** was the scene of an IRA terrorist outrage when a coach carrying soldiers and their families was blown up, killing 17. A plaque at the service station commemorates the murders.

HAWORTH [Bradford]

SE0337: 3 miles (5km) SSE of Keighley

Even if this Pennine town were not associated with, arguably, Yorkshire's most important literary family, it would still be worth visiting. Those who want to imagine mid-19th century northern England, the days of industrial expansion and the character of a place in the times of Dickens should come here. Despite the tourist attractions that have inevitably flowed from the Brontë legacy, we still see numerous **18th-century cottages**, which had housed handlooms and other machinery of the domestic system. We still see mid-Victorian shops, homes and public buildings in a collection rare in the county.

The principal thoroughfare, **Main Street**, is a cobbled hill leading from the earliest part of the town. At the bottom of the hill is the 17th-century Old Hall – now a hotel – and the even earlier Old

Fold Hall, both homes of the town's major family, the Emmotts. As we walk up the hill, look beyond the numerous book and antique shops and admire the old buildings before coming to the triangle of buildings where the streets of the upper town bisect. To the left is the **parish church of St Michael** which, unfortunately for Brontë fans, dates from 1880 and long after the famous family had all passed away. A look inside is worthwhile, however, but only the Perpendicular tower would have been familiar to the sisters and their austere father.

Despite its appearance, Haworth, like so many other isolated towns and villages in this part of the country, was populated by independent types who had little truck with outside authority, secular or spiritual. In the 18th century the place was considered a den of vice by the Church of England and vicars willing to go there were hard to find. Drunkenness and dissolution were common, not surprisingly perhaps considering the harshness of life on these moors and the complete disregard of the outside world. The famous Methodist churchman William Grimshaw brought some semblance of order. He was a Lancastrian who, in his younger days, had himself enjoyed a riotous career as a drinker and reveller. He came to Haworth in 1742 determined to impose the same sort of strictures on his flock as he had imposed upon himself; there was many an occasion when the fire-and-brimstone parson toured the town ready and willing to horse-whip any local lout he considered deserved it.

Close by the church is **Haworth Parsonage**, a place of pilgrimage for literary fans from around the world, and a 'must' on any visitor's list of priorities. Built at the beginning of the 19th century, it was to be the home of the Revd Patrick Brontë, his sickening wife Maria and their six children, who arrived here – with seven cartloads of furniture – from their last living at Thornton, near Bradford, in 1820. The house still echoes with the ghosts of those days. Many consider the lives of the Brontës to be tragic in the extreme; in fact, their lot was no worse than that of many in the Victorian era and much better than that of the labouring poor in Haworth and great mill towns a few miles away. Certainly the deaths of both Maria and Elizabeth at the ages of 11 and 10 respectively were tragic, but child mortality was high in those days. Mrs Brontë succumbed to cancer a year after the family moved in, and this must have greatly influenced the father's remote and gloomy mood. Despite all this, the surviving children, Emily, Charlotte, Anne and their beloved brother Branwell, had interesting childhoods. They were free to roam the moors around the town – still stunningly beautiful in all weathers – and had a privileged if not necessarily wealthy position in local society.

As was common in those times, the daughters of gentlemen were sent away to school, but not before

Brontë Parsonage, Haworth

the girls had begun to respond to their literary calling by producing small books and pamphlets for use in their nursery games. These, and masses of other material from later in their literary lives, are on display in the Parsonage and the new **museum** building which stands close by. The rooms where the family socialised, ate and slept are on view, and it is easy to imagine how life must have been in those days. The genius of the three sisters, achieved at first under male pseudonyms to fool the publishers, changed their lives and brought a greater prosperity. Haworth was an unhealthy place, however; the graveyard below the Parsonage was so overcrowded that it was declared a health hazard in Victorian times.

Tragedy struck the family in 1848 when their beloved Branwell, a slightly unbalanced young man whose undoubted artistic talents had been dissipated by drink and drugs, died at the age of 31. The three remaining sisters were devastated and just two months later Emily, author of *Wuthering Heights*, passed away after years of frailty. Anne, who wrote *Tennant of Wildfell Hall*, died at Scarborough six months later aged just 28. Charlotte, the eldest sister and the mainstay of the family, went on to write both *Shirley* and *Villette*, and in 1854 met and married her father's curate, the Revd A.B. Nicholls. The curmudgeonly old vicar refused to attend his daughter's wedding, and when Charlotte died less than a year later after catching a chill while walking on the moors, her husband was left to share the Parsonage with his father-in-law. The latter, far tougher than any of his talented children, lived on to the ripe, if not exactly happy, old age of 85.

A short stagger from the Parsonage is the **Black Bull** pub, a former coaching inn. This was the 'local' beloved by Branwell Brontë, who spent much of his time here – nearby is the old apothecary's shop where he acquired his opium, that essential attribute to the creative muse. The town's tourist information office is also worth looking into, not only for its booklets and leaflets; the premises were once the local **Yorkshire Penny Bank**.

HEADINGLEY [Leeds]

SE2836: 2 miles (3km) NNW of Leeds

There can't be many who don't know of this pleasant suburb of Leeds – or at least of its name. Home to **Yorkshire County Cricket Club** and scene of many a historic county or Test Match, Headingley not long ago faced the prospect of closure. Plans were developed to rebuild the ground near to the M62 at Wakefield. While this might have pleased those living south of Leeds, for whom the drive across the city to the ground is a tiresome journey, it failed to find favour with the YCCC committee and was finally abandoned. In a spirit of compromise, it was agreed that the antiquated Headingley facilities would be upgraded to meet the demands of cricket in the 21st century.

Once a grand Victorian suburb, complete with row after row of re-

spectable late 19th- and early 20th-century 'villas', Headingley fell from favour and now has a more 'studenty' feel about it. Smart shops and restaurants have begun to proliferate, however, and certain sections are once again becoming 'gentrified'. The **church of St Michael** on Headingley Lane was completed as recently as 1885 and is more impressive outside than in, thanks to its tall west tower capped by a thin spire.

HEATH [Wakefield]

SE3520: 1 mile (2km) SE of Wakefield

This really is a remarkable place. Close to the city of Wakefield, and yet a world away – a real treasure house of 18th-century architecture. We approach the settlement – it can't really be described as a village – on the road across the expansive **Heath Common**, a piece of land open to all since ancient times. Even today, people still make use of commoner's rights, grazing their horses amidst the gorse. For sheer wealth, the residents of Heath must have taken some beating. The first major building here, the **Old Hall**, has been demolished, but it was built in the latter half of the 16th century for the merchant John Kaye. It set the standard for all that was to come after it with its towers, grand mullioned windows and the latest in Elizabethan design touches. It is a tragedy that the building could not have been saved as commentators who saw it claim it to have been one of the most important

Elizabethan houses in Yorkshire. Interestingly, it was refuge at the end of the 18th century to catholic nuns fleeing the Terror in Revolutionary France. They are buried in the churchyard at **Kirkthorpe** not far away.

The Old Hall must have attracted the merchants of Wakefield who, in the 18th century, were already establishing large fortunes and reputations on the back of the town's place as a market centre and its prominence in the cloth trade. **Heath House** stands to the east of the site of the Old Hall and was begun in 1744 by James Paine. At the time he was just 21 but the building, complete with three bays and giant Ionic columns, illustrated the genius of the man who would soon be responsible for **Nostell Priory** just a few miles away.

Heath Hall stands on the same open green and is the work of John Carr. Although his later fame took him to Harewood House, Carr was born in nearby Horbury and this building was begun in 1754. It is a magnificent specimen of his work, with 11 bays and more Ionic columns. More modest cottages and a **Dower House** from the same period complete a remarkable ensemble. Not far away is the pub, the **King's Arms**, which is very atmospheric and with the original part of the building still lit by gaslight.

HEBDEN BRIDGE [Calderdale]

SD9827: 7 miles (11km) W of Halifax

This small town in the steep cleft of the Calder Valley is a classic example of a community which suffered a drastic decline in its traditional industries, only to emerge, phoenix-like, from the ashes. Hebden Bridge is now one of West Yorkshire's major tourist attractions, and rightly so, being filled with interesting shops, eating places and places to visit. The town is ancient, a traditional crossing point where the Calder and Hebden Water meet as they pour from the Pennines above, and the current **bridge**, although repaired several times, is believed to have been built in 1510. Even in those days, fleeces from the sheep which roamed these moors were being turned into textiles both in Hebden Bridge and in nearby Heptonstall. Both settlements had numerous weaver's cottages clinging to the hillsides, and many can be seen to this day. Once complete, the 'pieces' of cloth would be taken over the bridge by packhorse train to Halifax and other towns for sale in their cloth halls. By the 18th century, a certain amount of mechanisation was beginning, first with clothiers building homes for their weavers close to the power from tumbling streams. Many of these 'upside-down' houses, with storeys built as terraces along the gradient of the steep hills, remain and are highly sought after.

A century later, with help from the **Rochdale Canal** which cuts its way through the valley, came larger factories producing fine worsteds and corduroy as local specialities. It is still possible to travel along the canal from **Heb-**

Hebden Bridge

den Bridge Marina, either pulled in a horse-drawn barge or on a motorised narrow boat. The restored canal allows the visitor to be 'legged' through the dark **Fallingroyd Tunnel** and to enjoy the lovely Pennine scenery as far as Callis Wood and Todmorden. The work that made all this activity possible has now gone, but some of the old buildings remain with new uses.

This area was the cradle of the co-operative movement, which was founded just a dozen or so miles away – albeit over the border – in Rochdale. In 1870 the first co-op mill was built here as the Hebden Bridge Fustian Manufacturing Co-operative Society and all the workers shared in the profits of their industry. A mill that is worth visiting is **Walkley's Clog Mill,** be-

lieved to be the only clog factory in the world. Here you can see a clog museum, watch this traditional form of Pennine footwear being made and even buy a pair. And you thought clog makers went out with galleon builders! Lovers of the motor car will enjoy the **Automobilia Museum** on Billy Lane. The collection dates largely from the 1920s and 1930s and specialises in Austin and Morris cars; fans of the television series can see James Herriot's car.

Not surprisingly, a town as curious and ancient as this has its own interesting traditions, the most peculiar being the Hebden Bridge Dock Pudding Festival which takes place in May each year. Dock pudding is a delicacy peculiar to this part of the world and made from sweet dock, or bistort (not the stuff you rub on a nettle sting). Mixed with nettles, onions and porridge oats it is usually fried and served with bacon or sausages. Visitors wanting a little exercise will enjoy the **Hardcastle Crags Nature Reserve** further along the valley – a beauty spot in the care of the National Trust.

HECKMONDWIKE [Kirklees]

SE2124: 2 miles (3km) SE of Batley

A traditional woollen manufacturing town, in keeping with many others around it of similar style, Heckmondwike is a friendly, no-nonsense sort of place. It has few significant buildings, but one worthy of note is the massive **Upper Independent Chapel** built in 1890 for the Congregationalist sect. A massive portico and a domed tower give the building great, if undeserved, self-importance.

HELME [Kirklees]

SE1011: 1 mile (2km) N of Meltham

This is a rural hamlet which seems to have completely avoided any of the industrialisation which came to the area, including nearby Meltham and Marsden, in the 19th century. There are some remnants of the cottage industry method of textile production that was common across the county from the Middle Ages, but little else. The Brook family, who had business interests nearby, built the church in 1859. It is in memory of a son who died in his late 20s; tradition has it that on the day of his funeral a rainbow came out and the mourners agreed that a church should be built at its end. It is significant in that it has a wooden shingle spire, believed to be one of only two such constructions in the north of England.

HEMSWORTH [Wakefield]

SE4213: 6 miles (10km) SE of Wakefield

Once a prosperous market town, and in the 19th and the first half of the 20th century a bigger and even wealthier mining centre, Hemsworth is now a classic victim of the decline in the latter industry. Two decades ago there were half a dozen pits within walking distance of Cross Hill where the ancient market cross would have stood, now there are none. A general depression fell on the area in the 1980s, one which local people are doing their best to throw off. One method has been through leisure with the creation of the award-winning **Hemsworth Water Park**. Here, close to an ordinary Victorian park, the local town council built a remarkable complex of outdoor water sports attractions which is justly popular.

The **parish church of St Helen** stands on a slight rise above the main town. Although mainly dating from a reconstruction of 1867 there are elements dating from the 13th century, which indicate the importance of the area at that time. Just outside the town is the **Holgate Hospital**, founded in 1546 as almshouses by Archbishop Robert Holgate, a close ally of Henry VIII. He was born here in 1481 and rose to be Archbishop of York. The original buildings were replaced in the 19th century. In the town itself, Holgate also founded a **Grammar School.** It remains to this day – although the buildings are new.

HEPTONSTALL [Calderdale]

SD9828: 8 miles (13km) W of Halifax

As an example of a pre-Industrial Revolution manufacturing settlement, Heptonstall takes some beating. High up on the side of the Calder Valley, the village was from ancient times able to make use of the many strong and reliable streams which tumbled down from the moors above. Numerous small mills grew up, and many of the traditional weaver's cottages survive from the early 18th century and before. A cloth hall built in 1545 also survives. Cloth was taken down to the valley bottom on horseback, via the medieval cobbled 'Buttress'. With the coming of the large factories, Heptonstall's cottage industry suffered, but its population was able to make the daily trek down the hill into Hebden Bridge to work there.

As a result of these changes, the buildings of Heptonstall have been caught in a kind of time warp, making it of major importance for anybody interested in the development of architecture in this area. The **church of St Thomas** – or rather 'churches' for there are two in the same churchyard – can be dated to the 12th century, but with many of its features being of the later Perpendicular style. It was struck by lightning in the 1840s and a replacement built between 1850-54 in the same style. In the graveyard are two very different – but equally interesting – characters. The first is the notorious 'King' David Hartley one of the well-known Cragg Vale Coiners. This gang was active in the 18th century, 'clipping' the edges from gold coins and selling the valuable metal. Such activity was punishable by death and Hartley and his cohort were duly despatched at York in 1770. Clipping was common in those days and led to the 'milled' edging introduced at the turn of the 18th century. The other grave is that of the American poet Sylvia Plath, wife of Ted Hughes, who killed herself in disputed circumstances in 1963 at the age of just 31. He spent much of his early life in his hometown of Mytholmroyd.

Predictably enough, the Nonconformists were very influential in Heptonstall and their **Octagonal Chapel**, built in Northgate in 1764, is believed to be the longest in continuous use in the world. It is reputed to have been built in Rotherham and was brought here, piece by piece, on horse and cart. John Wesley is believed to have preached there many times. Its shape is said to have been chosen so that there should be no corners in which the devil could hide.

HEPWORTH [Kirklees]

SE1606: 1 mile (2km) SSE of Holmfirth

A pleasant moorland village with

many echoes of a past dominated by the daily struggle for survival against the elements and isolation, Hepworth has the usual collection of weaver's cottages, most of them dating from the 17th and 18th centuries. One local historian records that the village was once, probably in the mid 17th century, stricken by plague – a not uncommon blight in those days – and that local people buried their own dead in nearby fields to avoid spreading the contagion further afield. Focal point of the village is the local pub, **The Butcher's Arms**; originally several small cottages.

HIGH FLATS [Kirklees]

SE2007: 3 miles (5km) NW of Penistone

This small settlement beside the main Huddersfield road is, like its neighbour Birds Edge, a traditional farming community. How folk managed to eke a living at this altitude – it stands on the 1000ft contour – is remarkable. As well as sheep, which would have provided milk as well as wool and meat, people would have grown some barley and oats and perhaps raised a few vegetables. Even today, when the wind blows it can be chilly indeed. Particularly interesting, and down a lane with a sign to the Friends Meeting House, is a collection of 18th-century buildings which once formed the heart of a small **Quaker settlement**. The gathering is said to have begun meeting here in the mid 17th century, in a barn on the site of the present Meeting House.

In 1764 a Quaker boarding school was set up. Children would have lived here while their parents did missionary work in this country and abroad. Not far away, in Brockholes Lane at **Penistone,** a stand of trees and a plaque mark a now disused and lonely **Quaker burial ground**. Local historians also record the fact that Mill Bank House saw the opening in 1886 of a home for 'the restoration of inebriate women'.

HIGHTOWN [Calderdale]

SE1824: 1 mile (2km) S of Cleckheaton

Standing close to the village of Hartshead, this village was the first home of the Revd Patrick Brontë and his new wife Maria when the couple married in 1812. He was curate at Hartshead, but the couple lived here, at **Clough House**. There are also strong links in Hightown with the Quaker movement, apparently because the local landowner was converted by none other than George Fox when the latter visited the area in the 1670s. From then on a number of buildings were built for followers and areas of the village still bear the name 'Quaker'.

HIPPERHOLME [Calderdale]

SE1325: 2½ miles (4km) E of Halifax

There are interesting Elizabethan and Jacobean buildings in this village. Together with their mullions and sturdy appearance, they seem to have been here long enough to have become part of the gritstone landscape around them. While industrialisation came – and went – all around them, they give a good impression of what life would have been like in this area before the advent of the factories. Particularly important in their day were **Upper Rookes** and nearby **Rookes Hall**, both dating from the latter half of the 16ᵗʰ century. In neighbouring Coley, the **church of St John,** built in 1816 and one of the first 'Waterloo' churches, is worth a short visit.

HOLME [Kirklees]

SE1005: 3 miles (5km) WSW of Holmfirth

Right on the northern edge of the Peak District National Park, and with the Pennine Way just a couple of miles away, Holme is a lovely Pennine hamlet with marvellous walking country all around. Focal point of the village is a small triangular 'square' with stone setts and surrounded by late 18ᵗʰ -century two-storey cottages. Nearby is the local pub, **The Fleece**, which raises large amounts of money for the Royal National Lifeboat Institution. Although the cause is an excellent one, it is interesting that it should be the chosen charity of such a landlocked hostelry. The only water nearby is that which falls regularly on the moors, and is then collected by the attractive **Digley** and **Ramsden Reservoirs** nearby. There are picnic sites, parking areas and marked walks around both of these beauty spots.

The more adventurous can head for Holme Moss, part of the vast peaty expanse of Black Hill. Here the **Holme Moss television transmitter** stands amid stunning, if forbidding, scenery. Look out in the winter months for mountain hares. Introduced to the Peak District from Scotland in the 19ᵗʰ century they prosper here and are regularly seen dashing away from the feet of walkers. Brown like their lowland cousins in summer, the mountain hare turns white in the winter months – regardless of whether there is snow on the ground.

HOLMBRIDGE [Kirklees]

SE1206: 2 miles (3km) WSW of Holmfirth

The most remarkable feature of this small village is easy to see from the road which cuts through the valley on its way to Holmfirth from the high Pennine moors above. The valley sides are so steep that **cottages** were built, effectively on top of each other. Sometimes as many as four separate residences cling to the hillside, one above its neighbour – a kind of 19ᵗʰ-century tenement block with wonderful views. At the bottom of the valley, where the crossing of the River Holme gave the village its name, is the **church of St David,** which dates from 1840. The carved altarpiece shows scenes from life in this interesting valley and deserves a viewing.

Above Holmbridge stands **Bilberry Reservoir**, which in 1852, thanks to unusually heavy rainfall, saw 90 million gallons of water burst through the dam wall and thunder down the valley. Between here and Holmfirth 81 people were drowned – 44 of them in Holmbridge itself. A bible in the church, known as the Flood Bible, is a survivor of the inundation.

HOLMFIRTH [Kirklees]
SE1408: 5 miles (8km) S of Huddersfield

There can't be many who don't now know of Holmfirth, setting for the perennial BBC comedy series 'Last of the Summer Wine'. While the whole of the Holme Valley provides scenery and settings for the programme, this small town has captured the flavour of the programme and made it its own. Wandering around its cobbled and flagged streets it is easy to imagine Compo, Clegg and the others as they search – sometimes in vain – for the vigour of their lost youth. Near the imposing and blank-walled **church of the Holy Trinity** stands **Sid's Café**, which appeared in so many episodes. Once a dull and dismal part of town, shops have now sprung up all around and the dilapidated weaver's cottages – many of them three-storied – are being renovated and are much sought after. The **church** itself is interesting. One of few in the area from the 18th century, it was completed in 1787 after ten years of construction and has a sturdy tower and a triple-galleried interior. It replaced an older church badly damaged by a flood.

Everything about Holmfirth says this was a town where woollen manufacture dominated the scene, with the River Holme cutting through the middle and providing power for the machinery. The best way to see the place is on foot, dodging the innumerable coach parties that throng the town on summer weekends to gaze at **Nora Batty's house** and other scenes from the famous programme. As well as woollen manufacture, Holmfirth was also the home of one of England's more eccentric fads, the picture postcard. At the beginning of the 20th century, the opening up of seaside resorts thanks to the railways meant that most folk managed to get away, even if for just one day, to Blackpool, Morecambe or Scarborough each summer. The sending of postcards with sensible views of the resort or saucy cartoons, was the in thing – cheap and fun. The most famous postcard makers were Bamforths of Holmfirth (just check those old family albums and their name will dominate your collection).

Worth a look, is the gallery of well-known local artist Ashley Jackson whose television series advising beginners on how to paint has made him a household name. His evocative pictures, he is particularly good at representing wind and rain, sum up the moorland scene.

The Holme Valley has suffered five major floods; that of 1777 claimed three lives. The height of the floodwater is recorded on the wall of a shop in Station Road. The 1852 flood, which drowned 81 people, has its height recorded on a pillar close to the bus station. The **pillar** itself marks the signing of the Treaty of Amiens of 1801 and is known locally as 'T'Owd Genn' after its sculptor Henry Genn. Three people died in the last of Holmfirth's great floods: in 1944 after a cloudburst.

HOOTON PAGNELL
[Wakefield]

SE4808: 6 miles (10km) NW of Doncaster

If ever there was a 'time capsule' village, this is it. On the edge of the West Yorkshire coalfield, with grim and blighted landscapes all around, stands a small community more akin to the Cotswolds. Stroll through sleepy Hooton Pagnell and you almost expect Miss Marple to come cycling around the corner on a pre-war sleuthing mission. Built from local limestone, many of the buildings date back to medieval times and great effort has been placed on maintaining the historic flavour; houses rarely come on the market and those that do command justifiably high prices.

The **church of All Saints** dates back to early Norman times when the Conqueror gave the lordship of the manor to Sir Ralph de Paganel. Set high above the road, it requires 13 steps to reach the doorway. It boasts a great Norman arch and ancient door with original hinges, and there is herringbone masonry in the walls. Additions in the 13th

century make this a very pleasing building which unusually sympathetic restoration in Victorian times only helped to preserve. Marquetry from the 18h century adorns the pulpit. One interesting feature is the carillon, which plays a different tune every day.

Nearby **Hooton Pagnell Hall**, although surrounded by Victorian battlemented boundary walls, dates to the 14th century and boasts a gatehouse of that time. The building itself is as old with some important Tudor panelling. The village has a **market cross** dated 1253 and a cattle pound where straying animals would be kept until recovered on payment of a small fine. The village **cricket pitch** is a wonderful reminder of a more carefree time and competes with Nostell, a few miles away, for the beauty of its setting.

HORBURY [Wakefield]

SE2918: 3 miles (5km) WSW of Wakefield

Horbury, and its close neighbour Horbury Junction, have changed a great deal over the past century and a half. What we see now is a busy post-industrial town that once played host to one of the busiest **railway junctions** in the country, bringing with it the commensurate number of jobs. Back in the 18th century it was a quieter place, but one which no doubt basked in the limelight of being the birthplace of one of England's finest architects. Although known as 'John Carr of York', the creator of Harewood House and the master who improved Wentworth Woodhouse was born here in 1723. In 1791 he commissioned and built a new church for his hometown, at the huge cost in those days of £8000. This former jobbing workman had plenty of money, however – more than enough to finance his final memorial. When he died in 1807 he left no less than £150,000. His **church of St Peter and St Leonard** is a worthy classical building with a grand west tower and steeple complete with clock faces. Over the south door is a Latin inscription which reads, 'John Carr, architect, built this church at his own expense, in honour of God and for the love of his birthplace.' The great man is buried in the **crypt**. Another name worthy of note is that of Sabine Baring-Gould who was curate of Horbury from 1864 to 1867, during which time he wrote the famous hymn 'Onward Christian Soldiers'.

HORSFORTH [Leeds]

SE2337: 5 miles (8km) NW of Leeds

For a town so close to Leeds, Horsforth has managed to retain its own personal character and still has a 'villagey' atmosphere. There are plenty of individually run shops and most of the buildings are of a honey-coloured stone that seems to have avoided the soot that marred so many in the county during the dark days of industrialisation. The town grew up around a

ford over the river. Not far away in the valley of the Aire is Kirkstall Forge, where the monks from nearby Kirkstall Abbey smelted their iron ore. The **church of St Margaret** is a pleasant building completed in 1883.

The best-known citizen of Horsforth was Samuel Marsden, the 19th-century mill owner and factory reform campaigner. Another, and arguably England's first Marathon Man, was Foster 'Walking' Powell, who was born here in 1734. In 1773 he walked from London to York and back again – a distance of 400 miles – in 138 hours. The story goes that he cut three hours off that record a few years later and won £10 for his trouble. Powell was a phenomenon and much celebrated by the crowds who would line the roads as he walked by on his record setting attempts.

HUDDERSFIELD [Kirklees]

SE1416: 12½ miles (20km) SSE of Bradford

While its roots might stretch back in time to an age when a crossing was made here over the River Colne, much of Huddersfield's recorded history dates from the later 18th century onwards. Here, thanks to the local manorial family, the Ramsdens, came two canals and much business and prosperity. The **Huddersfield Broad Canal** is a short waterway linking the town with the older Calder and Hebble Navigation and terminating at **Aspley Basin**. The basin still stands and is well worth a visit. Across from the entrance of the Broad Canal is the start of the **Huddersfield Narrow Canal**. Opened in 1811, this route crossed the Pennines via the Standedge Tunnel at Marsden and drove on to the Tame Valley at the heart of industrial Lancashire. Some of the canal has been filled in, but a mile or so out of the town centre its towpath can be traced right up to **Tunnel End.**

The canals brought great prosperity for some, and hard, laborious work for others. Huddersfield was one of the country's centres of worsted and other woollen manufacture. The town's public and domestic buildings are almost exclusively no earlier than mid-19th century, but reward the visitor who is prepared to walk around and admire them. Perhaps the most interesting is the town's **railway station,** which was completed at the beginning of the 'railway age' in 1850. Along with St Pancras in London, it is probably one of the most interesting stations in the country, comprising an enormous eight-columned and porticoed entrance hall, flanked by colonnaded single-storey wings. Originally competitors, the Lancashire and Yorkshire Railway Company and the Huddersfield and Manchester Railway and Canal Company combined their interests here and together built this magnificent edifice – their company badges still adorn the building. Across the square on John William Street stands **Lion Chambers**, a grand building topped by a giant prowling lion. Standing there since 1853, 'Leo', as he is known, is reputed to get down from his vantage point and prowl the town's streets when the station clock strikes midnight. Conveniently, the station clock does not strike.

A walk through the busy town centre brings us to the **parish church of St Peter** which, although built on a Norman foundation, was rebuilt to its present grand design in 1836 by J.P. Pritchett of York. The same architect was responsible for the station and the Lion Chambers. The church is Perpendicular in style, with a splendid tower. The **town hall**, another in the grand Victorian style, boasting of the town's wealth and power, stands on Princess Street and was completed in 1881. These days it plays host to the world famous Huddersfield Choral Society which each year organises an international standard season of musical events.

Huddersfield Art Gallery on Princess Alexandra Walk houses a permanent exhibition, much of it British and mostly tracing the period 1850 to the present day. Artists represented include Henry Moore, L.S. Lowry and Francis Bacon. The town's main **museum** stands in **Ravensknowle Park** on Wakefield Road, just outside the town centre. The **Tolson Memorial Museum** stands in a mid-19th century villa in the grounds and contains much material devoted to

Huddersfield's woollen heritage. There are also exhibits of items unearthed by archaeologists at the nearby Iron Age fort on Castle Hill. In the park stands an interesting **clock tower**, built here as a memorial to those who fell in the First World War. The structure comprises columns taken from the town's dismantled Cloth Hall of 1798. Another, much grander Great War memorial can be seen on the other side of the town in **Greenhead Park**.

Huddersfield has a whole list of famous names to its credit, perhaps the most famous being the Labour Prime Minister Harold Wilson. Other sons and daughters of this university town include Roy Castle, the Star Trek actor Patrick Stewart and the businessman Lord Hanson.

IDLE [Bradford]

SE1736: 3 miles (5km) NNE of Bradford

Not the most generous title to give a place, but this town was a hive of industrial activity in the last century. The relative youth of Idle as it is seen today means much of the architecture is of the familiar Victorian vernacular style so common in the West Riding. **The Church of the Holy Trinity** in Town Lane was built between 1828-30, one of hundreds constructed with so-called 'Waterloo Money' following the Napoleonic Wars. The Church of England, slow out of the blocks but eventually acknowledging the growth of towns in the industrial north and Midlands, set aside money to build new places of worship in towns such as Idle. Non-conformists, particularly Methodists and Unitarians, already had a hold though and competition for flocks would continue unabated well into the 20th century.

If it is inspiration you are after it can be found in the story of Joseph Wright. He was born in the neighbouring village of **Thackley** in 1855 and at the age of six got a job leading a donkey cart to and from the local quarry. Later he went to work in a woollen mill and then began a night school for his ill-educated peers. He saved enough money to go to Germany, took a degree at Heidelburg and wrote a book on German dialects. Not content with this success, he returned to England and became professor of comparative philology at Oxford and compiled the six-volume *English Dialect Dictionary* in 1905. The book was created on two million slips of paper and Wright had to publish the thing himself, no publisher would touch it. It is a classic of its kind and his name is revered by all who love dialect and local history.

ILKLEY [Leeds]

SE1147: 4 miles (6km) W of Burley-in-Wharfedale

There can't be many Yorkshire folk, nor visitors to the county, who have not visited Ilkley. But this now lively and interesting town was not always so. Until the 18th century and the interest in 'water cures' it was but a small village on the banks of the River Wharfe, with towering hillsides on both sides.

A natural site in the range and the nearby river have ensured man's presence since time immemorial. In Roman times there was a **fort** here, called Olicana, with a road crossing the Pennines to Manchester. Experts reckon the fortress covered two acres, but there is nothing to see today. A later Anglo-Saxon settlement made its mark, particularly in the **church of All Saints.** This building is largely Perpendicular in design, with some 13th-century features, including a dog-toothed south doorway. An unusual Jacobean font cover can be seen, and there is an interesting assembly of monuments and family tombs from that period and from Elizabethan times.

Most noteworthy, however, is the trio of **Anglo-Saxon crosses** that stands inside the church near the tower. One, remarkably, still has its original head, and all are covered in designs of great intricacy. The tallest of the three has the Four Evangelists carved on the back, with a figure of Christ on the front. A number of beasts, together with scrolling vines, make up the ensemble. This and the middle-sized cross are thought to be from the 9th century, while the smallest – complete with an angel and more beasts – could be as early as 700. Together, historians agree, they make up the most important collection of Anglo-Saxon crosses in the north of England.

Close by, in Castle Yard, is the 16th-century **Manor House,** a museum dedicated to explaining life both in the period when the house was built, and Ilkley's more ancient history from Roman times.

While a few homes and farm buildings in the area can be dated to the Tudor period, it was as a Georgian and then Victorian spa town that Ilkley rose to fame and fortune. Known as the 'Malvern of the North' it owed its success to a spring of moorland water at **White Wells** just above the town, and rich clients in search of a cure for gout and other ills would be taken there on the backs of donkeys. A stone shelter and bathhouse still stand – with a Victorian story of its haunting by tiny figures dressed in green adding a little frisson to any visit there.

In the 1840s, with the opening of the Hydro at nearby Ben Rhydding, Ilkley entrepreneurs opened their own hotels, spas and health centres in the town, while the railway only added to customer interest. At the same time mill owners and other successful businessmen from Leeds, Bradford and other Yorkshire towns built grand homes here, away from the smog and grime their factories created; many still stand in and around the town.

This rapid growth saw the building of **St Margaret's Church** in 1878 by Norman Shaw, the great Victorian architect responsible for New Scotland Yard in London.

Ilkley's wide streets and fine shops leave the visitor in little doubt that this town is a cut above most and it remains a popular residence for folk working in Bradford and Leeds. Visitors should not, however, confine their day to the town alone – not when there is **Ilkley Moor** to explore.

This large stretch of wild moorland, with a number of names including that of the town intermingling on the Ordnance Survey maps, is a delight. The views down to Ilkley and up Wharfedale are stunning, but it is man's ancient connections with the place which delight. A number of stone circles can be found on the moor, together with other pieces of gritstone carved with 'cup and ring' devices dated back to Celtic times (1000BC). Most remarkable of all, and again dating back to ancient Britain's mysterious pre-history, is the **Swastika Stone** bearing the design that then symbolised the destructive element of fire. The swastika is a symbol familiar to many cultures, its name coming from the Sanskrit word 'svasti' meaning 'good fortune', and has been found as far afield as India.

We can't leave the moor without reference to the song which is synonymous with it – 'On Ilkla Moor Baht 'At'. Sung in broad Yorkshire, this ditty was coined in the 1870s and tells the story of a young man seen on the moor courting a lass named Mary Jane. His friends warn the Romeo that venturing into such wild country without headgear will see him catch his 'death o' coud'. The result will be that his body will be eaten by worms, the worms by a duck and the duck – inevitably – by his friends. It concludes 'then we shall have gone and etten thee'. QED.

JACKSON BRIDGE [Kirklees]

SE1607: 2 miles (3km) SE of Holmfirth

If ever there were a 'typical' Pennine village, this is it. Gritstone cottages crowd the hillside and appear to tumble down to the beck in the valley bottom. Almost all date back to the 18th and 19th centuries, and many bear all the signs of once housing handloom weaving frames.

Woollen textile production had for centuries been an occupation for the whole family, and this was only disrupted and then destroyed in that form from the middle 1700s onwards. Prior to that, wool would be spun by hand, and then woven on handlooms in the long upper gallery of these three-storey cottages (at the back there would be a 'taking-in door' for bringing wool and cloth in and out of the weaving chamber).

Once woven, the cloth would have to be 'fulled' to thicken the fibres, then washed and hung out to dry on rows of posts known as 'tenters', from the Latin for 'stretch'. The cloth would hang from hooks; hence the phrase 'on tenterhooks'. Some cottages had their own area for this process, in other villages several cottages shared the same open space.

Also worth a look in Jackson Bridge is the pub, the **Red Lion.** This is 'Last of the Summer Wine' country and the exterior of this hostelry features in many a scene from the popular TV series. Take a peek inside and the walls – where not covered with horse and other brasses – are festooned with photographs and other mementoes of Foggy, Clegg and Nora Batty.

KEIGHLEY [Bradford]

SE0641: 8 miles (13km) NW of Bradford

Not a long way from the Lancashire border, this town which grew up where the Rivers Aire and Worth meet is Yorkshire through and through. What is interesting though is that, contrary to popular myth, cotton was worked in Yorkshire, and in Keighley in particular. Production of cotton textiles alongside woollens was always a feature of Keighley's manufacturing character; and together they made the town rich and prosperous. But the success came with a heavy price. Local folk used once to be known by their neighbours as 'Keighley kay-legged-uns' a disparaging description attributed to the days when poor diet and lack of fresh air and sunlight led to rickets and other disabling ailments among the mill workers.

There has always been a settlement here, but in 1801 the town's population was just 5750. A mere half a century later it had grown tenfold, with huge numbers coming here from the surrounding countryside and beyond to find work in the mills and shelter in the thousands of terraced homes which sprang up. Some of the former still survive, a few of them even producing textiles, and many of the terraces from the later Victorian era give the town great character.

In a back-handed compliment if ever there was one, architectural historian Nikolaus Pevsner says of Keighley, 'Compared with other industrial towns in the West Riding, it strikes one as spacious, clean and friendly.' It is all these things and boasts a fine collection of Victorian public and commercial buildings which Mrs Gaskell and perhaps even the Brontë sisters will have known. Most of them are on the wide **North Street,** which still bustles with shops and stores. It was built as a turnpike road in 1792 and widened in 1882. Along here is the **Town Hall Square,** again dating back to the days of Queen Victoria.

The **church of St Andrew** is dated 1848 and its large size shows how economically important the town had become by this time. There is a grand west tower and a feeling of scale about the whole structure. Another North Street landmark is the **Roman Catholic church of St Anne** which was opened eight years earlier. It was the work of the renowned architect of Birmingham's Roman Catholic Cathedral, August Pugin.

If Keighley's terraced houses give a good impression of how mill workers lived in West Yorkshire a

East Riddlesden Hall, Keighley

century and more ago, there are a number of grand homes on the outskirts of the town which speak just as eloquently of the lifestyle of their employers. One that is open to the public was built as Cliffe Hall in 1832, a home for the cotton barons the Butterfields. Its remarkable design harks back to Tudor times. Fifty years later, another Butterfield greatly enlarged the building, giving it the modest new title of **Cliffe Castle**. It passed through other hands before finally coming into the ownership of the local authority; it is now **Keighley Museum** and is signed just off the A629 Skipton road. Visitors are treated to a vast array of exhibits, from local geology to natural history, from the town's industrial heritage to rooms furnished in the grand, chandelier-adorned, Victorian drawing room style. One item of particular interest is the loom and other artefacts from the home of Timmy Feather, Yorkshire's last handloom weaver who lived and died in the nearby hamlet of Stanbury.

Keighley is also the home base of the justly renowned **Keighley and Worth Valley Railway**, the town's station being the first on the line which works its way up the valley to Oxenhope, calling at Haworth on the way, using marvellously restored and cared for steam locomotives. Also at the station is the excellent **Vintage Railway Carriage Museum,** which has a good collection of exhibits. Audio presentations bring the vehicles to life and tell the story of rail passenger travel in the great days of steam. Memorabilia and other items are available in the large shop.

KIPPAX [Leeds]

SE4130: 2 miles (3km) S of Garforth

There must have been a thriving settlement here long before the Norman Conquest if the splendid **church of St Mary** is anything to go by. Built to an Anglo-Saxon ground plan, it is one of the finest Norman churches for miles around. The masonry is of the herringbone style throughout, giving a pleasing and unusual appearance. There are no aisles and the west tower, nave and chancel are Norman. They provide students with a perfect case study of this important period in English history. The font is from the 1660s and there is an interesting Anglo-Saxon cross fragment to be seen. This has a standing figure with outstretched arms, and intertwining serpents.

KIRKBURTON [Kirklees]

SE1912: 4½ miles (7km) SSE of Huddersfield

This attractive village was in earlier days a busy centre for both coal mining and woollen manufacture. It is a quieter scene today, with many residents commuting to Wakefield, Leeds and Huddersfield for their employment.

Of particular interest to the visitor is the **church of All Hallows** in largely Early English style. Built about 1200, it has fine lancet windows, but the most interesting feature is the west door. It has large dog-tooth carvings, a transition from the earlier Norman motif so common in English church doorways, and combines them with four-petalled flowers – a pleasing ensemble. The tower is later by probably two centuries and has some Victorian additions to the top. More 19th-century changes appear inside the church, but in essence it is a very early church and significant for that fact alone. Interesting benches with bobbin ends date from Elizabethan and Jacobean times, with some even earlier.

The name All Hallows comes from All Saints' Day, 'hallows' being the Old English 'halig' or holy man or saint. This dedication to Christian martyrs falls on November 1, the day before being All Hallows' Eve, or Hallowe'en.

KIRKHEATON [Kirklees]

SE1817: 3 miles (5km) NNE of Huddersfield

Here the **church of St John** appears at first to be a building of the late 19th century, the type of structure many would pass by. But closer inspection reveals much more interest. While the nave, aisles and west tower are Victorian, there is a chancel chapel of Perpendicular heritage housing the final resting place of the Beaumont family, squires of the locality for centuries. A number of interesting monuments, particularly from the 17th century, can be studied here, including one in brass. Also in the church is a long 13th-century coffin lid carved with shield and sword.

In the churchyard is a sad **memorial** to 17 children who died in 1818 in a mill fire at nearby Colne Bridge. Less maudlin is another grave memorial, this time in the shape of a barrel, marking the last orders of a well-known local toper.

KIRKLEES [Calderdale]

SE1622: 4 miles (6km) NW of Mirfield

This tiny settlement, close to the thundering M62, is more interesting for what once stood here than for what the visitor may see today. In the 12th century, Cistercian nuns built a **priory** here. Evidence on the ground where the buildings, including a chapel, once stood suggests it was never as large as some other ecclesiastical centres in the county. At the Reformation, records show it had just seven nuns. All that remains is the decaying mullioned **gatehouse,** which the experts believe was built in the 16th century. In its prime it had substantial oak beams, some of them intricately carved.

Yorkshire has plenty of associations with the legendary **Robin Hood**, indeed, perhaps even more than Nottinghamshire and Derbyshire combined. One legend says that while fleeing the hated Sheriff of Nottingham he took refuge at **Kirklees Priory** where the prioress, his aunt, was expected to shelter him. The story says that the prioress, considering the rebellious Robin a menace to society and the established order in which she thrived, while pretending to 'bleed' him for some ailment, succeeded in killing him. Before he expired, he is supposed to have blown his hunting horn to summon the faithful Little John and then, with his help, to have fired his last arrow into surrounding woodland. Where the arrow fell, he was buried. One story says the site was the place of an **ancient standing stone**, again mixing fact and myth and harking back to Britain's pre-Christian times. The site is still shown as 'Robin Hood's Grave' on Ordnance Survey maps.

Nearby **Kirklees Hall** was built at the end of the 16th century in the Jacobean style. The building is in an E-shape and surrounded by Kirklees Park.

KIRKSTALL [Leeds]

SE2636: 3 miles (5km) NW of Leeds

Leaving Leeds in a westerly direction on the A65 Ilkley road, we suddenly come upon what is probably the best preserved Cistercian monastery in the country. **Kirkstall Abbey** now finds itself in what is little more than a suburb of outer Leeds – when it was built it stood in a heavily forested valley beside the River Aire. In the 12th century Leeds was a tiny village and the river clean and full of fish, an ideal setting for a monastic order seeking peace and tranquillity. The monks who founded Kirkstall in the 25 years up to 1175 had come here from their mother monastery at Fountains Abbey in North Yorkshire. Interestingly, their first choice of a site had been at Barnoldswick (pronounced 'Barlick' by those in the know) on the other side of the Pennines. Lancashire's loss was Yorkshire's gain. Despite the ravages of the Dissolution in 1540 and the industrialisation of the 19th century, the abbey is remarkably well preserved, its buildings almost complete and its tower and walls generally reaching to their original heights.

The visitor, therefore, is in no doubt about how grand this place would have been in its heyday, housing dozens of holy brothers and employing hundreds of illiterate lay brothers. Not surprisingly, the latter did all the heavy work in a medieval monastery, while the better-educated monks prayed eight times a day. Interestingly, the Cistercians – or 'white monks' due to the colour of their habits – had split from their stricter founding Benedictine order so that they could spend more time working and studying. In the first half of the 12th century they established numerous abbeys, granges and other religious centres across England, including another Yorkshire abbey at Rievaulx.

The abbot Aelred of Rievaulx wrote in the 1100s of what the monks were trying to achieve when they created their great houses, 'Everywhere peace, everywhere serenity, and a marvellous freedom from the tumult of the world. Each thing seems to belong to all, and all to each. No perfection expressed in the gospel is wanting to our order and our way of life.'

Immense wealth came from their farming of sheep. So much so that the order dominated the wool trade which brought England gold from the continent. The fortunes of cities such as Ghent and Bruges in Belgium depended upon their manufacture of English wool. Lower down the Aire, in the direction of Leeds, the monks also worked iron, the preserved **Kirkstall Forge** providing evidence of this industry.

Cruciform-shaped Kirkstall Abbey's vast size is evidence of the order's wealth and power. While the main religious building and its neighbouring chapter house are fascinating, the lay buildings all around are also extremely interesting. Here we get a good view of what life must have been like. There is a well-preserved infirmary, refectory where meals would have been taken, kitchen and malt house (the monks liked their mead and ale).

Across the main road is the gatehouse, important parts of which also date from the construction of the abbey. It was once the residence of rich local iron masters and is now the home of the **Abbey House Museum**. Here are three streets of shops and cottages recreating life in Victorian Leeds, including a pub, ironmonger's shop and a grocer's, a pipemaker's workshop and a chemist shop. Children will particularly enjoy the exhibits of old toys and can even play old-fashioned slot machines using pre-decimal copper pennies.

Beside the road is an interesting obelisk-shaped **milestone** which tells us the vital information that we are exactly 200 miles from London – and from Edinburgh. The **church of St Stephen,** built in the first half of the 19th century contains the grave of Richard Oastler, the tireless campaigner for factory reform. Although incarcerated in the infamous Fleet Prison for debt, he continued to campaign for an improvement in the conditions of work, especially those faced by young children.

KIRKTHORPE [Wakefield]

SE3621: 2 miles (3km) E of Wakefield

Once a separate village, now a suburb of Wakefield, Kirkthorpe boasts an attractive Perpendicular church devoted to **St Peter.** In the churchyard are the graves of several nuns who fled France during the Terror of the Revolution at the end of the 18th century. The style is Perpendicular throughout and dated to the 15th century. Look out for the rare Jacobean poor box, about the only thing in that period to help the destitute. Speaking of which, the Elizabethan **Frieston's Hospital Almshouses** provided shelter for four male inhabitants. The rooms open into the dining hall.

KNOTTINGLEY [Wakefield]

SE4923: 2½ miles (4km) NNE of Pontefract

This was until recently a prosperous mining town but, as with all the others in the area, has suffered due to the collapse in the price of coal and the closure of the pits.

Chemical works nearby do provide employment for a goodly percentage of the population. The **church of St Botolph** has a nave which was rebuilt in the 1700s, but the lower part of the tower shows the true period of the building to be Norman (look for the characteristic round-arched window). Pevsner, the cruelly honest architectural historian, described the Victorian stained glass as 'hideous'. Take a look and decide for yourself.

LAYCOCK [Bradford]

SE0341: 2 miles (4km) W of Keighley

Not far from Keighley and a stone's throw from the famous hamlet of **Goose Eye,** Laycock is little more than a main street stretching for almost a mile beside the main road. Interestingly, perhaps because it is so close to the Lancashire border, cotton spinning made up as significant a part of the manufacturing economy last century as wool. As is so often the case, this hillside village had plenty of weaver's cottages prior to this date, but probably the oldest house in Laycock is the **Manor House** on Main Street. Mullioned and transomed windows date it to the end of the 17th century.

Local historians delight in the tale of William Sharp who, in 1807, was stood up at the altar – his curmudgeonly father had fallen out with the bride's family. Poor William was so traumatised by this experience that he went home to bed – and stayed there, not saying a word, until his death in 1856! Not surprisingly, by then he was a huge man who had to be crated up and lowered into his grave by an eight-strong funeral party.

LEDSHAM [Leeds]

SE4529: 2½ miles (4km) N of Castleford

Just inside the West Yorkshire border and situated between the A1 **Great North Road** and the **Roman road** (A656), this small village stands above the flood plains of the River Aire. Although now a commuter village, Ledsham was an agricultural centre until a few decades ago and seems largely untouched by the coal mining and other heavy industry just a few miles to the south across the river.

Anglo Saxon doorway, All Saints Church, Ledsham

It would be worth coming here just to sample the quiet atmosphere, and the welcome and ale on offer at the excellent local pub, **The Chequers**.

But there is more here, of the kind church aficionados would travel 100 miles to see. There are more than a few churches in the West Riding which bear the evidence of Norman workmanship, but few – if any – which show as much of Anglo-Saxon heritage. The **church of All Saints** is a wonderful building thought by the experts to date from the 8th century – in other words from when the Vikings were sacking York! The nave, the base of the tower and chancel arch all show evidence of being built then in the walls of rubble which would once have been faced by a limestone based plaster. Now it is easy to see where Anglo-Saxon ends (especially in the tower) and Norman begins, and once again where the Perpendicular work of the 15th century takes over in the uppermost part of the tower and the spire above. Windows are largely Victorian, but there are fragments from the 15th century. The monuments are also well worth close examination, one of them in white marble. The most interesting is that to Lady Elizabeth Hastings by the celebrated Peter Scheemakers. 'Lady Betty', as she was known, lived nearby at **Ledston Hall**. Although a noted beauty at the start of the 18th century, she never married, choosing instead to help the poor and invest in education. The daughter of the seventh Earl of

Huntingdon, her tomb records that, 'She dispensed justice, honour, truth, so earnestly and sincerely and candidly that she won for herself a name more lofty than any inscription can record, more lasting than any monument.' Sir Richard Steele, first editor of the *Tatler*, which he founded in 1709, wrote of her, 'To love her is a liberal education.' What on earth did he mean? She founded an orphanage nearby in 1721.

LEDSTON [Leeds]

SE4328: 2½ miles (4km) NW of Castleford

The aforementioned Lady Betty lived in this village, just a mile away across the fields, in her family home of **Ledston Hall** (private). There, with two spinster stepsisters, she made a number of alterations to what is in essence a house of the later 17th century. The history of the hall goes back much further, however, as the monks from Pontefract Priory had a 'grange' here in the 12th century and in the following century built a chapel, some of which survives in the later building. The main hall of a medieval building can also be identified, together with a considerable amount of additional structure from the 16th and 17th centuries.

LEEDS [Leeds]

SE3034: 9½ miles (15km) NNW of Wakefield

As with Bradford, this volume can only scratch the surface of what a city the size of Leeds has to offer. The following is merely an over-view of a marvellous metropolis well worthy of close study. Unlike Bradford, Leeds was an important town from the earliest times and received a market charter in 1205. By the time of Elizabeth it was one of the West Riding's main woollen cloth trading centres, and a century and a half later the visitor Daniel Defoe was able to comment on its prosperity and clamour. Leeds had two traditional cloth halls where weavers would come to trade their freshly woven 'pieces' of cloth, but it was not so much the manufacture of textiles as their conversion into useable garments and other products that made the city's fortune in the 19th century. Alongside a plethora of other trades, Leeds – Yorkshire's most populous city – became a centre for the production of clothing, with numerous factories and workshops springing up across the city.

As in earlier times, prosperity came from the River Aire and its **wharves,** and worked its way from here – close to the modern railway station – up **Briggate** (or 'bridge street'), culminating in the **Headrow**. To the west of this highway the city grew, first slowly as former burgage plots were infilled, then rapidly as unsanitary courts and closes were built to house the labouring poor of the early decades of the Victorian era. One or two remain, including **Swan's Yard**, site of the **City Varieties Music Hall** and setting for the television programme 'The Good Old Days'. Before then, rich merchants

City Hall, Leeds

had already laid out impressive Georgian terraces, as at **Park Square,** which still exist as expensive office suites. What we see now, however, is very much a Victorian city; one of the most important in the Empire, and with buildings to match.

Most impressive amongst these, standing in all its glory on the Headrow, is the grand **town hall**. Built in the 1850s, it has an unusually long, columned and porticoed front, guarded by white – if eroding – lions. This magnificent example of Victorian public design set the scene for other great town halls, including those of Rochdale, Bolton and Manchester across the Pennines. The building was as much a public statement as a place of civic decision-making; then and now it says 'successful – and proud of it!' It remains the home of the in-

ternationally renowned Leeds Piano Competition.

Across the road, and balancing it perfectly, are the Victorian **City Library** and then the **City Art Gallery**. This lovely, airy structure close to the **Cenotaph** is reached via a grand staircase topped by a work by Yorkshire sculptor Henry Moore. Additional works by Castleford-born Moore are found inside, plus others by Wakefield's Barbara Hepworth and Jacob Epstein. The same collection of buildings also includes the **City Museum**, bursting with exhibits from all over the world. Behind this collection of buildings is the interesting **City Hall**, constructed in the 1930s with two giant golden owls on the roof. The owl, two of which appear on the city's seal – between a heavily fleeced sheep – appeared on the arms of Sir John

Saville, Leeds' first alderman in the early 17th century.

The development of Leeds as a hive of industry perhaps made it inevitable that little remains from the pre-Victorian age in the city centre proper. One noteworthy building is the **church of St John the Evangelist** in New Briggate. Built in the 1630s, it is an extremely rare example of the period, with a magnificent interior and exceptional woodwork in the pews and pulpit. Interestingly, and more evidence of the importance of textiles even at this early date, the church was built on the orders of John Harrison, a cloth merchant. Not far away, on Boar Lane, is the **church of the Holy Trinity**, this time of the 18th century with a tower added in the style of Sir Christopher Wren in 1839.

Another splendid feature of Leeds – and a magnet for the dedicated shopper – are its Victorian and Edwardian arcades. These elaborate tiled and vaulted structures, where the consumer can forage protected from the elements, have now all been restored to their former glory. The city was particularly proud that investment in these renovations recently led to the top London store **Harvey Nichols** choosing Leeds as the location of its only branch outside the capital. Not far away, and on a similar principal of keeping the customer protected from the elements, is the remarkable **Kirkgate Market**, the work of Leeming and Leeming, the same architects behind the indoor market at Halifax.

Also on a commercial front, it is worth remembering that in the 1880s Leeds was the place Marks & Spencer began their now world famous 'Penny Bazaar'.

As well as the museums around the town hall, Leeds has others well worthy of the visitor's attention. On the south bank of the River Aire, in an area which was once run-down but is now rising from the ashes of dereliction is the marvellous **Royal Armouries Museum**. Here we find examples of arms and armour from around the world and across the span of time. The Royal Armouries, based at the Tower of London, looked long and hard before choosing Leeds as the place to display the vast quantities of material in its collection. What makes the museum so interesting, however, are not the valuable items in the glass cases, but the opportunity to learn how they were used at first-hand. Dramatic interpretations of battle diaries, demonstrations of arms and armour, and event jousting tournaments are all offered to the visitor. It offers a full day out for everyone.

Down the road is the famous **Tetley Brewery**, complete with its own **Brewery Wharfe** visitor attraction. Here, visitors learn the art of brewing from costumed actors, meet the famous shire horses and – of course – sample a pint of the excellent brew.

Across the river, on the site of the former Quarry Bank Flats, is the **West Yorkshire Playhouse**, one of the country's most modern and best-respected theatres. Looming

82

Towns and Villages of Britain

above it is **Quarry House,** home to the Department of Health, a modern building of truly Stalinist ghastliness and a blight on the cityscape.

On the other side of Leeds, on Beckett Street and close to St James's Hospital (known to all as 'Jimmy's'), is one of the best new museums in the county. The **Thackray Medical Museum** is based in the former Leeds Workhouse and gives the whole family a comprehensive look at health and medicine down the ages. Appalled by the awful conditions in a Leeds slum of Victorian days, we follow the great medical pioneers as they fight against disease and ignorance. Later, a tour of the body's organs has the children amongst us enthralled.

Leeds is also home to the world's oldest railway. **Middleton Railway** was built as a horse-drawn trackway linking this small village with the River Aire in the 1750s. It thrived as a waggon-way until, in 1812, John Blenkinsop and Matthew Murrary developed steam locomotives on the line. It predated the Rainhill Trials and the Liverpool to Manchester Railway by almost two decades. A short stretch can still be travelled thanks to a trust which runs steam engines on the line from Moor Road Station.

LINDLEY [Kirklees]

SE1118: 3 miles (5km) NW of Huddersfield

This is a gritty West Yorkshire mill village if ever there was one. Now part of the urban sprawl which is Huddersfield, it still has a characteristic community feel and is still dominated by the kind of patriarchal benevolence of the Victorian age. The local landmark is the village **clock tower** built in 1902 by James Nield Sykes who owned the local wire works. Cynics – and they probably aren't wrong – reckon this act of public goodwill was more than an ego trip on behalf of Mr Sykes; after all, if his workers could see the clock, what excuse would they have for being late? The structure has a sculpture with the theme, naturally enough, of Time, accompanied by the virtues of Justice, Love, Purity and Truth. **St Stephen's Church** is a typical 'Waterloo Fund' creation with little particular merit, although the nearby **Methodist church** dates from 1745 and is one of earliest in the county.

LINTHWAITE [Kirklees]

SE1014: 3 miles (5km) SW of Huddersfield

Standing above the **Huddersfield Narrow Canal**, Linthwaite is a typical settlement which grew up thanks to the industry brought by the waterway and by the turnpike road across the Pennines which appeared half a century earlier than the canal, in the middle of the 18th century. Like so many others, this small settlement was still producing woollen textiles using the age-old 'domestic system' until local merchant George Mallinson built his first mill in 1857 and changed the lives of local people for good.

Buildings of interest include the lancet-style **Christ Church**, finished in 1828, and another church built with funds allocated by the Church of England to ensure the word of God could be heard in the industrialised north and Midlands. Up the hillside is **Linthwaite Hall**, built around 1600 in an L-shaped design with the typical mullioned windows of a well-to-do yeoman farmer's home. Further on is **Blackmoorfoot Reservoir**, an important stopping-off point for migrating wildfowl and wading birds.

LINTON [Leeds]

SE3846: 2 miles (3km) SW of Wetherby

Linton Hall is now an upmarket hotel, complete with swimming pool and other sporting facilities, but was built in the late 17th century. Linton is centred on a lovely village green and both a packhorse bridge and a 'clapper bridge' cross the River Wharfe. The latter design is ancient and involves slabs of stone, some standing vertically in the water, with others laid on top to create the bridge itself. Also in this pleasant village is the Early English **church of St Michael,** close by **Linton Falls**. Dated at around 1300, the church has a short bell turret with a pyramid roof. Inside there is much evidence of Norman work, especially in the arcades and the chancel arch.

LOTHERTON [Leeds]

SE4436: 3 miles (5km) NE of Garforth

Just off the A1, the remarkable **Lotherton Hall** is a classic Edwardian building created by the Gascoignes, a local landowning family who made a fortune when their land in the West Yorkshire coalfield gave up its wealth in the 19th century. The building is now run by Leeds City Council and is well worth a visit. Displays of treasures include an important collection of Chinese pottery and other related items in the **Oriental Gallery**, costumes and important paintings and furniture from the art nouveau period.

The gardens are one of the hall's finest features and include a recreation of a William and Mary garden laid out in the Dutch style of the 17th century, plus areas reflecting the Edwardian history of the house. Another attraction, and particularly popular with children, is the extensive collection of rare and endangered birds ranging from flamingos to snowy owls and hornbills. Also in the grounds is **Lotherton Chapel**, which dates back to Norman times.

LUDDENDEN [Calderdale]

SE0424: 3 miles (5km) W of Halifax

You deserve a pint if you can say the name of this South Pennine town the first time without tripping over your tongue, or perhaps two if you can manage **Luddenden Foot** a mile or so away down the valley! Indeed, it was a pub, first called The Swan when built in the 17th century and then changed to its present name, the **Lord Nelson**, which for years served as one of the main public buildings of Luddenden. Until the coming of the mechanised textile industry in the middle of the 19th century, Luddenden was little more than a collection of houses at the stone bridge crossing the narrow River Luddenden. It was a stopping-off point for merchants and travellers on the relatively safe low-level route between Lancashire and West Yorkshire.

One local family, the Murgatroyds, who helped establish the importance of woollen manufacture, built a grand stone house here in the middle of the 17th century. **Kershaw House** is a typical yeoman's mansion in the style of many 'Halifax Houses' which still dot this part of the country. It has a rose window in the two-storey porch and fine transomed windows. James Murgatroyd was an avid collector of homes, a hobby that culminated with his acquisition of the splendid **East Riddlesden Hall** near Keighley. The **church of St Mary** was built in 1817 and altered in the 1860s, when the congregation was on the increase and money was available for improvements.

The coming of rail transport led to a line through the valley, and a station was built at Luddenden Foot with mills and homes springing up around it. The dissolute Branwell Brontë, troubled brother of the famous sisters, was station-master here for a time. As the Industrial Revolution forged ahead, more and more woollen, silk, worsted and cotton mills sprang up; greatly increasing the local population and bringing welcome prosperity. Much of the manufacturing activity has now long gone, but the area is attractive to commuters working in the major towns and cities on either side of the border.

LUMBUTTS [Calderdale]

SD9523: 2 miles (4km) E of Todmorden

This tiny village is probably more visited by walkers than by motorists due to its location on the South Pennine watershed, just a mile or so from the **Pennine Way**. In Victorian days the weaver's cottages here – and a number still stand – were made redundant by the inevitable construction of several woollen mills. The mills have now all gone, but a remarkable **water tower**, which provided them with power, remains. Three waterwheels, one on top of another, would have stood in the 104ft high tower and powered Lumbutts Mill, one of several round about owned by the great Todmorden wool barons, the Fieldens.

MANKINHOLES [Calderdale]

SD9623: 3 miles (5km) SE of Todmorden

Like its sister village of Lumbutts, Mankinholes is a remote and sometimes forbidding place. When the mist is down on the tops, the settlement seems lonely and cold. But when the sun shines in early summer, the walker on the nearby Pennine Way or the ancient stone-flagged causeways (pronounced 'causeys') which once kept the feet of packhorse drivers out of the winter mud, should be tempted to look around. Many of the houses date from the 17th and 18th centuries, when this was a small but prosperous settlement where the population spun, wove and raised a few sheep and vegetables. Now caring owners who travel out of the village for their work have saved the properties from ruin. While Methodism was strong throughout the West Riding, Quakerism was prominent too, and in Mankinholes this was especially true.

On the hillside above the village is a local landmark well worth visiting. The granite tower of **Stoodley Pike** was built in 1815 to commemorate the victory of the Duke of Wellington at Waterloo. Superb views down towards Rochdale and on to the Lancashire plain are just reward for tackling the ascent.

MANNINGHAM [Bradford]

SE1534: 1 mile (2km) NW of Bradford

Once a village standing alone above the slightly larger settlement of Bradford, Manningham was all but swallowed up when industrialisation came in the 19th century. Now little more than a suburb of Bradford, and in parts in something of a decline, its principal attraction to the visitor was built in 1873. **Manningham Mills**, built by local woollen magnates, the Listers, is an awe-inspiring structure. The self-confidence with which the owners allowed architects to adopt an Italianate design for a woollen mill is remarkable. The 250ft **chimney** is reminiscent of that built a few years earlier at nearby Saltaire, but this illustrates the power of the northern factory owner in every brick.

MARSDEN [Kirklees]

SE0411: 3 miles (5km) W of Meltham

Marsden must always have been an important town on the high and sometimes dangerous route across the Pennine watershed between Lancashire and Yorkshire. The first town at the western extremity of the Colne Valley, it would long have been a stopping-off point for the packhorse trains that would have come over the 'top' laden with goods.

The main obstacle was the exposed and miry **Marsden Moor**. Nowadays, much of this wild and hauntingly beautiful countryside is in the care of the National Trust. Merlins, a rare bird of prey anywhere in the country, breed on the Marsden Moor Estate, as do wading birds such as redshank and curlew. In the 17th century, packhorse trains of up to 40 ponies would have come this way on a route known as **Rapes Highway**, built to carry wool, coal, iron, salt, lime and cloth down into the High Peak of Derbyshire. A **bridge** at

Eastergate would have carried these trains and is dated to the 1650s. A better route was built in 1765 by John Metcalf, known in the history books as 'Blind Jack of Knaresborough'. This turnpike builder was responsible for hundreds of miles of road, and dozens of bridges in Yorkshire, Lancashire and Derbyshire. Despite being made blind by smallpox at the age of six, he was able to survey his roads by feeling his way using a walking stick. As if this were not achievement enough, he was a remarkable athlete and horseman and in 1746 fought at Culloden. On Marsden Moor he 'floated' his road on rafts of heather to prevent the surface sinking into the peat. Marsden was also the last town seen by narrow boats using the **Huddersfield Narrow Canal** before they entered the **Standedge Tunnel** on their way to Diggle three miles away.

Nowadays, the town is an interesting collection of 18th- and 19th-century buildings, including the late 19th-century **church of St Bartholomew,** with a somewhat unkempt graveyard. At the beginning of the 19th century, however, it was the scene of some of the bloodiest incidents in the revolt against the growth of mechanisation in the textile industry. The Luddites, men whose livelihood was based on the traditional cottage industry method of cloth production, saw destitution rear its head when new machinery came into their world. Not surprisingly, some rebelled, and in a series of incidents in the

early 1800s machines were wrecked and mills burnt. In Marsden, the forging firm of Enoch and James Taylor made cropping frames which, although not as expert at trimming cloth as the men who did it by hand, were much quicker and much cheaper. Local Luddites took hammers to the frames, the hammers – or 'Enochs' – being made by the same firm and leading to the saying 'Enoch has made them – and Enoch shall break them'. One local mill owner, the outspoken William Horsfall, was shot and killed by Luddites on his way back to Marsden from Huddersfield.

Marsden also has a place in the history of North America as the home of Henrietta Thompson, mother of General James Wolfe. Wolfe, who was born in Kent, took Quebec from the French in 1759 after scaling the Heights of Abraham; he died in the hour of victory.

MEANWOOD [Leeds]

SE2837: 2½ miles (4km) NNE of Leeds

Although now a suburb of Leeds, Meanwood was once a village in its own right, owned and farmed by the monks from nearby Kirkstall Abbey. The main attraction to the visitor today is **Meanwood Park** and the neighbouring **Hollies Park**. Together, these provide a lovely area of open space close to the city centre: a haven both for picnickers in summer and wildlife all year round. The **Meanwood Valley Trail** leads to here from

Golden Acre Park, another of Leeds' horticultural treasure houses.

MELTHAM [Kirklees]

SE0910: 2½ miles (4km) S of Slaithwaite

It is clear from the number of industrial buildings on and close to the main road through the village that Meltham was once a thriving, bustling place. Nowadays, much of the silk and other manufacturing that went on here has gone, but it is a pleasant Pennine settlement. The most interesting building is the church of St Bartholomew, which was founded in 1651 at the height of the English Civil War. Unfortunately, the only remains of that church are a date stone in the porch and some mullioned windows used in a cottage opposite. The building we see now dates from the 1780s, with the tower being added in 1835. One of the monuments is to a member of the Brook family, big employers in Victorian times when they ran the local thread mill. It was they who built Meltham's town hall.

METHLEY [Wakefield]

SE3926: 5 miles (8km) NE of Wakefield

Had it not been much restored, as per the Victorian fashion, in 1876, the church of St Oswald would be one of the most important churches in this part of the Yorkshire. As it is, and despite the 'improvements', it is still well worth a visit for what it shows us of the transitional nature of architecture in English churches in the 13th and 14th centuries. Parts of the building are in the Decorated style, others Early English and the remainder is Perpendicular from the later 15th century. Most interesting of all is the fine collection of funerary monuments, the oldest being from the 1400s and continuing up to the 19th century. Here are buried several members of important families, including the Watertons, the Saviles and those of the Earls of Mexborough. Some of the armour and clothing is superbly done and provides an object lesson in the finery worn by the rich at the time of the Wars of the Roses.

Look out for the magnificent lectern, believed to be Dutch and dated to around 1500, and the pulpit that was made for the church in 1708. Also important is the stained glass in the south chapel. This also dates from the 1400s and comprises eight figures and eight angels.

MICKLETHWAITE [Bradford]

SE1041: 3 miles (5km) E of Keighley

This is an interesting and attractive village on the southern side of Rombalds Moor above Bingley. Despite the inevitable industrialisation brought in the Victorian era, many of the buildings date from the 1600s and 1700s, giving the place an older 'feel' than many others in the area which have little of their early history left. Happily, a goodly part of the village is now a protected conservation area. **Micklethwaite Grange** and the **Manor House** both have interesting histories and both date from the 17th century when small scale agriculture and spinning and weaving at home would have put bread on most tables. The families of better off yeomen would have occupied these two buildings.

Standing close to the Leeds and Liverpool Canal, **Holroyd Mill** was built in 1810 for cotton spinning. It was later used for woollen weaving. Nowadays it is a craft centre with a variety of trades represented.

MIRFIELD [Kirklees]

SE2021: 3 miles (5km) SE of Dewsbury

The **church of St Mary** has an interesting history. Built in the 13th century, it was rebuilt in 1825, and again in 1871 by the great Sir George Gilbert Scott. Unusually, the **tower** from the original church has been preserved and stands close by its successor in the church grounds. A round **pier**, dating from 1200, stands in the new church vestry.

MORLEY [Leeds]

SE2627: 4½ miles (7km) SW of Leeds

A typical woollen town which found prosperity in the second half of the 19th century, Morley is still a busy place today. Although close to Leeds, it still has enough individual character to support two weekly newspapers. Romantics claim the town was built, like Rome, on seven hills, but several of them have been excavated over the centuries for the excellent gritstone from which they are made. The **town hall**, designed on the lines – if not the scale – of Leeds Town Hall, was built at a cost of £41,000 and opened in 1895 by locally born Herbert Asquith. The Liberal politician was first Home Secretary and in 1908 became Prime Minister. He faced host of major constitutional issues such as home rule in Ireland and the Suffragette movement, and he also led Britain into the war in 1914. He headed a coalition war cabinet until 1916, when Lloyd George ousted him.

Another of Morley's famous sons was Sir Titus Salt, born here in 1803 and creator of **Saltaire** near Bradford half a century later.

MYTHOLMROYD [Calderdale]

SE0125: 5 miles (8km) W of Halifax

A tongue-twister if ever there was one, this is a typical Pennine mill town which would once have rung to the clamour of numerous mills. Now, they are gone, but the landscape which inspired one of Britain's greatest poets remains and the place is now a place of pilgrimage to the late Poet Laureate, Ted Hughes. He left Mytholmroyd in 1937, at the age of seven, for Mexborough in South Yorkshire, but there is no doubt that the wild moorland of his birthplace influenced his work. Hughes married the American poet Sylvia Plath. When she committed suicide in

1963 she was buried at nearby Heptonstall. He said little of their relationship, and particularly her death, until the publication of his acclaimed volume of poems 'Birthday Letter' when he was dying of cancer in 1998.

NETHERTHONG [Kirklees]

SE1309: 1 mile (2km) NW of Holmfirth

Driving up the hill from Holmfirth, itself an archetypal Pennine settlement, one comes to a remarkable time warp of a place. Sister village to Upperthong, there are numerous 17th- and 18th-century stone-built **weaver's cottages** here, most with three storeys, the topmost being set aside as one long room in which a loom would have stood. A look around the back reveals the 'tekkin in door' by which wool and cloth would be moved. In some cases these doors and the staircases leading to them are still extant, others have been filled in.

The Church of All Saints was built in 1829, but as so often elsewhere, the 'chapel' was just as important in the 19th century for the large percentage of Nonconformists in the community. As larger woollen mills began to be built in Holmfirth, local people would track downhill each day for work. Those who could find none were committed to 'the Bastille', a three-storey building which still stands today – a kind of mini-workhouse in which families were split up and the miserable inhabitants employed in soul-destroying tasks.

NETHERTON [Kirklees]

SE1213: 2 miles (4km) SW of Huddersfield

The main building of distinction in this quiet village is, as so often in England, its church. **St Andrew's** is new by most standards, but remarkable in design and well worth the short detour from Huddersfield. Designed in 1881 by J.D. Sedding, it was described by that expert yet amateur lover of all that is good in English architecture, John Betjeman, as 'small but most original'. The bellcote on the west front, with two buttresses, is what makes it stand out from the ordinary, with the poet likening it to the much earlier chapel on Lindisfarne, or Holy Island, in Northumbria.

There was coal mining in the vicinity as early as the 15th century, providing much employment and leaving familiar scars on the landscape. The recently closed **Denby Grange Colliery** was linked underground with Caphouse Colliery a few miles away at Overton. The latter is now the **National Mining Museum for England**. Nearby is the Calder and Hebble Navigation, one of the earliest canal-cum-river widening schemes, which carried the coal to other industrial centres. First came the Humber Keel barges, then, at the end of the Victorian period, short, stumpy, rounded barges known as 'Tom Puddings'.

NEWMILLERDAM [Wakefield]

SE3315: 3 miles (5km) SSW of Wakefield

A small community nestled along the sides of the sweeping S-bend in the main Barnsley to Wakefield road, Newmillerdam comes complete with several pubs, craft shops and other attractions. The reason is not its pleasant appearance as a community, pleasing though that is, but the feature which gives the settlement its name: a corn mill is thought to have stood close to the site since the 1200s, but a new mill was built here in the 1820s.

The large **lake** standing off from the road is now a country park in the care of Wakefield Borough Council, and must be one of the most visited in the county. Park in the large car park on a Sunday morning, and compete with dozens of others to walk the dog, jog or feed the large numbers of wildfowl that winter and breed here. During the rest of the week it is less crowded, and even more attractive. A path surrounds the water, and in many places branches off into mature woodland and then pine forest. Kettlethorpe Hall, an 18th-century mansion built by the Pilkington family and standing some distance back from the water, once owned the land. Best-known former resident was Caroline Norton (1800-1875), granddaughter of the Restoration playwright Richard Brinsley Sheridan, inventor of Mrs Malaprop in *The Rivals*. Mrs Norton married a dissolute barrister in haste, to repent at leisure. She took up poetry to support him and her three sons, but in 1836 left her husband. He brought an action of 'criminal conversation' (adultery) against the Whig Prime Minster Lord Melbourne. The case against Melbourne, mentor to the young Queen Victoria and himself the cuckolded husband of Lady Caroline Lamb (the latter's obsession with Lord Byron was the scandal of the age), was thrown out as without foundation. Separated from her spouse, she promoted women's rights, protested against the evils of the factory system and wrote a large amount of poetry, including 'The Arab's Lament to his Steed'.

An interesting feature from this period, or rather moved to the site around this time (1842), is the elaborate **boathouse** beside the path. The crumbling yet elegant facade comes from the **Bridge Chapel** at Wakefield. Restoration of the important chantry chapel by Sir Gilbert Scott saw the stone brought here and incorporated into this lovely folly.

Nearby, on the other side of the main road, is **Seckar Woods Local Nature Reserve**. This beautiful old woodland was once owned by the Wentworth family of Wooley Hall. Today, after opencast mining in the 1840s, it is a mixture of dry heath, covered in heather; and wet heath, abundant in mosses, lichens and rare sedges. Together with mature woodland, this provides a varied and rich habitat for insects, birds and other wildlife. The reserve is one of five Sites of Special Scientific Interest in the Wakefield Borough.

NEW FARNLEY [Leeds]

SE2431: 4 miles (6km) SW of Leeds

Considered a separate community from Old Farnley, home of the magnificent John Carr masterpiece **Farnley Hall**, New Farnley grew up at the very beginning of the Victorian era. Four sons of wool merchant James Armitage founded the Farnley Iron Company in 1844 and brought in workers from Bradford. The place had a strong Nonconformist tradition and is now a commuter village for both Leeds and Bradford.

NORMANTON [Wakefield]

SE3822: 3 miles (5km) NE of Wakefield

Never one to restrain himself when he thought it appropriate to stick in the knife and turn it, architectural historian Sir Nikolaus Pevsner described Normanton as, 'A large, drab, colliery village or town, lacking in village as well as urban properties.' That was in 1959, and although as grossly unfair then as now, the visitor has to look a little harder than usual to locate Normanton's charms.

The last century and a half brought the town growth, jobs and prosperity. It also brought pollution, some poor housing, and in recent years recession. The steel and mining industries that provided jobs for thousands have now both gone, with little to show in their place.

But Normanton is a historic site, believed to date back to the 600s, with a name given to it by the Vi-kings, who called it 'Northmannatun' or 'town of the Northmen'. An **earthwork** of possible Roman origin stands nearby, offering a vantage point towards the River Calder and Wakefield.

The **church of All Saints** is much restored in the Victorian style. Its blackened exterior says much about the quality of the air here until the middle of the 20th century. The building is largely Perpendicular in style, with one or two earlier features including a Decorated chapel and nave arcades. Especially notable is a pillared funerary **monument** to John Freeston, an Elizabethan lawyer who dedicated a grammar school to the town's youngsters.

NOSTELL [Wakefield]

SE4018: 3 miles (5km) NW of Hemsworth

This tiny hamlet on the main Wakefield to Doncaster road has always had a rural air about it, with a number of farms in the locality. Until about 15 years ago a reasonable amount of work was provided by the now, inevitably, closed colliery.

A colony of monks, sometimes described as 'hermits', lived in the area in pre-Norman times. Devoted to St James, they were befriended by Ralph Adlave, friend and confessor to Henry I who fell ill at Pontefract on his way to Scotland with his king. Hunting in the area during his recuperation, he met the monks who had presumably been attracted there by the fish to be found in the natural lake that is still a feature of Nostell.

Ralph was given permission to establish them as a regular priory of Augustinian canons dedicated to St Oswald, or 'Oswi' as he was known when, as king of Northumbria, he was killed by the pagan Penda of Mercia at Oswestry in 642. A charter of 1121 gave the canons permission to build a church on the site, almost certainly containing a relic of the saint. The name St Oswald lives on in the title of the owners of the great house that now stands here.

Another **church** was built outside the confines of the monastery in the 16th century. A Protestant Prior, Robert Ferrer, built it. When Queen Mary acceded to the thrown he was burnt at the stake for his trouble, but the building, much affected by mining subsidence, still stands. In 1530, while it was still without a roof, the Archbishop of York, Cardinal Wolsey, confirmed 300 people here after being summoned back to London by Henry VIII. The **church of St Michael and Our Lady** is attributed to the neighbouring hamlet of **Wragby**, but while the locals might concern themselves with the distinction, the visitor will see one community. Of Perpendicular design, the church stands in the grounds of the great house. It has a much older Norman font. In the early 19th century, a remarkable collection of mid-European, largely Swiss, painted glass was acquired and held in the church. In recent years, due to subsidence, the collection

has been removed for safekeeping, with some of it on display in the house. Monuments to the ennobled Winn family, including the creator of Nostell Priory, Rowland Winn, are worth examination.

The village has one of the prettiest **cricket grounds** in West Yorkshire.

Most visitors come here to see **Nostell Priory**, one of the most important 18th-century houses in the country. The estate was owned by the Winn family, who had an earlier house on the site and had made their fortune in the previous two centuries as drapers to Queen Elizabeth and the nobility.

The fourth baronet, Sir Rowland Winn, had completed a European Grand Tour when, in 1733, he ordered the construction of a house in the grand Palladian style. Much influenced by what he had seen on the Continent, Sir Rowland, then just 27, commissioned James Paine to work on the designs. Even in a period when men made their mark early, Paine was ridiculously young – just 19 – when he began work on a design drawn up a few years earlier.

Despite, or perhaps because of his youth, Paine's creation is a remarkable structure set off by wonderfully landscaped grounds. Thirty years later, with work still going on, the fifth baronet brought in a usurper to Paine's crown – another thrusting youngster, Robert Adam. His interiors at Nostell are stunning, but he also brought his skill to work on the outside of the house as well.

Now in the care of the National Trust, although the St Oswald family still live at the house, Nostell Priory is a marvellous structure set in lovely parkland and well worth a day's visit. There are stunning pictures, including the 16th-century 'Family of Sir Thomas More' and 'The Procession to Calvary' by Pieter Breughel, a grand collection of Brussels tapestries and one of the finest collections of furniture by Otley's Thomas Chippendale.

In the grounds are the remains of the **cock-pit**, used in the 1700s for cock-fighting, an **ice house** hewn into the bedrock and a number of other intriguing architectural features.

NOTTON [Wakefield]

SE3413: 2 miles (3km) NW of Royston

This tranquil village between Wakefield and Barnsley appears in the Domesday Book of 1086 as 'Notune', 'the north settlement'. It has a rural air, which belies the fact that beneath it and all around is evidence of mining. Ilbert de Lacy, Lord of Pontefract Castle, held the land hereabouts. His successors later ceded it to the monks of Monk Bretton, near Barnsley, and those of Nostell Priory a few miles away.

In the 18th century Notton and its land became part of the vast Wentworth estates, and were heavily mined from Victorian times onwards. After the last war, when the estate was broken up, the villagers bought the village green for £5. Notton and the surrounding area is now popular with commuters and homes command premium prices.

Notton Park is a wooded area with evidence of occupation dating back to the Iron Age.

OAKWORTH [Calderdale]

SE0338: 3 miles (5km) SE of Keighley

This tiny town in the Worth Valley now receives most of its visitors via the service of the excellent **Keighley and Worth Valley Railway.** The volunteer-run scenic railway runs between Keighley and Oxenhope. **Oakworth Station** is particularly worth visiting in the winter, when it is lit exclusively by gaslight. Film fans will recognise it as the setting for the popular 1960s movie *The Railway Children*, featuring Jenny Agutter.

If you visit by car, look out beside the Colne road for Oakworth's **Holden Park,** once the site of the home of Sir Isaac Holden, one of several inventors each credited with devising the Lucifer match. Not satisfied with this, Sir Isaac, a Scot by birth, did much to revolutionise the process of wool-carding and made himself a huge fortune in the process from factories in Bradford and in France.

Obsessed with healthy living, he built dozens of hothouses in the grounds of his home to supply himself with fresh fruit and vegetables all year round. The story goes that each morning he breakfasted on a baked apple, a biscuit, an orange and 20 grapes. It must have been good for him: he was 90 when he died in 1897.

When he wasn't eating or being a Liberal MP, he was busy spending £120,000 on **Oakworth Hall**. He produced a Winter Garden with a Turkish bath fed by water from reservoirs specially built nearby. Lots of the main buildings have gone, but the gardens survive, together with grottoes and other interesting bits of garden construction.

OSSETT [Wakefield]

SE2920: 3 miles (5km) W of Wakefield

This typical industrial township bears all the marks of the Victorian era when its prosperity was based on woollen manufacturing and the 'shoddy' or rag reclamation trade. Evidence of this increase in wealth, and population, is the **Holy Trinity Church,** built in 1865 in the Gothic style, with a spire reaching 226ft into the sky and visible for miles around.

A notable son of Ossett is Stan Barstow, whose realistic 1960s novel *A Kind of Loving* forever altered the views others had of the northern working class.

OTLEY [Leeds]

SE2045: 2½ miles (4km) NE of Guiseley

This is a lovely market town at the mouth of Wharfedale and historically linked with that valley. Not surprisingly, it was once both a market town and a centre for wool trading, but here factories never took over and the market has survived to this day in the old market square. As at Pontefract, there is also an old **Buttercross** where farmers would sell their dairy products, protected by a solid roof from wind, rain, and – occasionally – the heat of the sun.

The **church of All Saints** is grand and imposing, evidence that the town has been an important and wealthy trading centre since the Middle Ages. While there are some Norman features, the bulk of the church is 13th and 14th century. The altar rail is unusual and dates from the end of the 17th century. Most important of all though is the large collection of **Anglo-Saxon crosses**, many with interesting carvings ranging from foliage to a dragon, a large bird and even human recreations. Look out, too, for the Viking grave-slab.

There are a variety of tombs and monuments, including one to a Longfellow who is believed to have been an ancestor of the 19th-century American poet Henry Wadsworth Longfellow. Another interesting family with tombs in the church is that of Fairfax. The family hail from **Denton** further up Wharfedale, but many lie at rest here. Most notable member of the dynasty is Thomas Fairfax who commanded the Parliamentary horse corps at Marston Moor in 1644. He defeated Charles I at Naseby the following year, but retired from active service in 1650 and Cromwell was appointed commander-in-chief. Fairfax headed the delegation that, in 1660, arranged for the return to England of Charles II.

Of great interest, across Church

Lane, is the monument to the 23 'navvies' – or navigators – who died digging the 2¼-mile (4km) rail tunnel beneath Bramhope Moor between 1846 and 49. The **Tunneller's Monument** is a small-scale version of the entrance to the tunnel itself – both are masterpieces of the Golden Age of British engineering.

Another famous son of Otley is Thomas Chippendale who was born in 1718, the son of a joiner. Apprenticed as a cabinet-maker, he particularly specialised in chairs made from mahogany – the dark, hard wood was only recently entering the market from South America. Among the many grand homes that still contain some of his highly prized work are two in West Yorkshire: Nostell Priory, near Wakefield, and the magnificent Harewood House. A statue of the great craftsman still stands in Otley today.

Another work of art, this time more substantial, is the seven-arched medieval **bridge** over the River Wharfe, beside which stands **Wharfemeadows Park.** This is a very popular spot on a summer's day with plenty of attractions for children, together with boating and other activities. Nearby is the site of the Wharfedale Agricultural Show, revered as the longest established in England and dating back to 1796. It takes place every May; get there early to ensure time to look around properly.

There is a grand view of Otley from the elevated hilly ridge above the town, known to all as the

Chevin. This lovely wild area now includes the 280-hectare (700-acre) **Chevin Forest Park,** a gift to the people of Otley from a local landowner, and comprising woodland and rocky crags. Man is believed to have crossed the area for thousands of years with one route, named Yorkgate, believed to have once been the road linking York with Tadcaster and Ilkley.

Evidence of stone quarrying now proves attractive to climbers. In 1830 the workings provided the foundations of the Houses of Parliament. Bridlington Pier and Scarborough Marine Drive also took stone from the Chevin. The area is a local nature reserve, with information available from the ranger base at the former farmhouse known as the White House.

OULTON [Leeds]

SE3628: 5 miles (8km) SE of Leeds

This is a small village between Leeds and Wakefield which has grown considerably in the last few decades as former agricultural land has been turned over to housing for those working in both cities. Landmarks include the **church of St John** built in 1829 by Thomas Rickman, who before turning to his craft was in turn a chemist, grocer, doctor, cornfactor and insurance agent. Externally, it is one of his finest buildings, in the neo-Gothic style with lancet windows and a needle-shaped steeple. It stands in the grounds of **Oulton Hall,** built in 1850 and now a hotel and conference centre. Not far away is an early 17th-century house with black and white walls in the 'Tudor' fashion.

Oulton's best-known son is the scholar Richard Bentley. Born to poor parents in 1662 he nonetheless managed to get an education at Wakefield Grammar School and then went to Cambridge. His skills in the Classics were legendary and he ended up as master of Trinity College in 1700. Notorious for his arrogance and overbearing nature, he quarrelled incessantly with his peers, and at one point misappropriated university funds to do up his own house.

OXENHOPE [Bradford]

SE0335: 4 miles (6km) SSE of Keighley

At the end of the **Keighley and Worth Valley Railway,** this former mill town clings to the side of the Pennines like so many others in this harsh, yet appealing landscape. In excellent walking country, the best way to see it is to take the train from Keighley and tramp the moors above the town.

In Oxenhope itself, the **church of St Mary** is interesting for the way its Victorian architects copied the early Norman style of eight centuries earlier and managed to avoid adding the almost inevitable bits and pieces from their own fussy times.

PONTEFRACT [Wakefield]

SE4522: 2½ miles (4km) SE of Castleford

Whether famous for its now un-

fashionable liquorice sweets, its racecourse or its castle, Pontefract, once known as 'Tanshelf' is a place which should be on every visitor's 'must see' list. A settlement has probably stood on this site since Roman times, the close proximity of the junction of the Rivers Calder and Aire making human habitation almost inevitable.

Principal among the places to visit is **the castle,** which dates from Norman times when William the Conqueror gave huge tracts of land in Yorkshire to his fellow robber baron Ilbert de Lacy. He built a wooden fortress on the hill where the present castle remains stand, a fortress which his descendants turned to stone in familiar motte and bailey plan the following century. The curtain walls still survive, along with the foundations of several towers. The visitor can also make out the plan of a **small chapel** dedicated to St Clement, and also on view are the kitchens, with two large bread ovens, the remnants of stables and other buildings. Of particular interest, and usually open to the public, are **cellars,** once used as underground magazines, in the middle of the castle site. These were used to house prisoners during the three sieges the fortress underwent during the Civil War.

Indeed, it was the Civil War which led to the destruction of the castle, both during the conflict and afterwards when it was 'slighted', as the language of the times quaintly puts it, by Cromwell to prevent it ever again providing a base for his opponents. A painting of the castle in the early 17th century by Keirincx gives the best impression of how the building would have looked in its heyday and is reproduced in the visitor centre. The original hangs in **Pontefract Museum** on Salter Row in the town centre.

If the battles between the Cavaliers and the Roundheads were not enough, Pontefract Castle already had 500 years of bloodshed in its history. After the de Lacys, the castle passed into the ownership of the house of Lancaster and Earl Thomas. Unfortunately for him, he quarrelled with Edward II, and after losing the Battle of Boroughbridge in 1322 was brought back to his own castle, tried for treason and beheaded on nearby Sir Thomas's Hill.

Other residents over the centuries included the all-powerful John of Gaunt, Richard III while Duke of Gloucester (the north country was always his political homeland) and Charles, Duke of Orleans who was here as a prisoner after the Battle of Agincourt in 1415. Most infamous of all, though, must have been the imprisonment of King Richard II by usurper Henry Bolingbroke (later Henry IV). How Richard died is unknown; Shakespeare claims he was killed by an axe during a fight, others that he starved himself to death or was murdered in the night. What is in no doubt is that by January 1400 he was dead; the population doubted it so much his body had to be carried in open procession to London, for all to see.

Not surprising that the Bard should have forever lumbered it with the title 'Bloody Pomfret'.

The Civil War sieges that finally led to Pontefract Castle's destruction in 1649 also did much to ruin the neighbouring **church of All Saints.** This former parish church was badly damaged in the fighting, with the Puritans happy to let it remain so. Nonetheless, a goodly proportion of the 14th- and 15th-century building still stands with the central tower of particular interest. It wasn't until 1838 that anything was done to revive the building and make it once again useable.

While All Saints was out of commission, the folk of Pontefract worshipped in **the parish church of St Giles,** beside the marketplace and in the middle of the town. Its classical lines date from the early 1700s and remind one of the many Wren-era churches built in London after the Great Fire. The west tower was rebuilt in 1793.

Nearby is the **Buttercross,** which was built in 1734 as a shelter for the sale of dairy produce on market days. Its columned structure is still used today and provides a pleasant focal point at the west end of Market Place. This is the oldest part of the town, with names of some alleyways and snickets dating back to medieval times. In the middle of Market Place is the old **Market Hall,** opened in 1860, while at the east end stands the **town hall.** This Georgian building, with an arcade at ground floor level, was built in

1785 on the site of the old Moot Hall.

The **Museum** on Salter Row in the town centre is worth a quick visit, and provides a useful overview of the development of the town and castle. Pontefract was once famous for its liquorice and one of the displays is dedicated to the history of this Mediterranean plant and its role in the town's history. Pontefract Cakes, stamped with an image of the castle, were first made in 1760 by a local chemist, although the history of liquorice growing in the town is most likely rooted in medieval times when monks may have grown it as a medicinal plant. The **Valley Gardens** on the edge of town were once liquorice fields and the last commercial crop was grown in the town in 1966.

Salter Row was the northern side of the vast medieval market square, and the poorer end at that – just take a look at the street names. Ratten Row means 'rotten' and Pudding Middens was the dump for offal from butchers in the Shambles (where the Market Hall now stands).

Another curious remnant of this town's colourful history is the **Hermitage** below Pontefract General Infirmary in Southgate. Founded in 1368 and first occupied by a 'Brother Adam', it consists of two rooms cut deep into the rock and accessed via dozens of stone steps. Check with the museum as to its occasional opening hours.

On the outskirts of the town, close to the M62, **Pontefract Race-** course is believed to be the longest, continuous circular flat racecourse in Europe.

POOL IN WHARFEDALE [Leeds]

SE2445: 2½ miles (4km) E of Otley

No prizes for guessing the river on which this attractive village now stands. The Wharfe, flowing strong here in winter as it rushes out of the dale, is crossed by **Pool Bridge,** built in 1793 and widened in 1815. Before then, travellers had to use a ford of the river, a potentially hazardous exercise for at least half of the year.

Not so long ago, Pool was a small settlement, having originally grown up towards the end of the 18th century thanks to a fulling mill beside the river. Later came a paper mill, which provided employment right up to the early 1980s. Nowadays the town, just three miles (5km) from **Leeds-Bradford Airport**, is largely a commuter base for those who work in these two cities.

Of note is **the church of St Wilfred,** built in 1839 when the village was expanding, which boasts some fine stained glass.

PUDSEY [Bradford]

SE2233: 4 miles (6km) E of Bradford

This town must have been a polluted, bustling hive of activity a century ago. Then, not only woollen mills, but also shoe factories, a candle works and other industries were all carried on by the folk who lived in the crowded folds and yards which made up the majority of the housing. One such fold, **Booth's Yard**, has now been restored and turned over to commercial activity, along with the nearby yard which has found a new role as a shopping mall.

Many famous names are associated with Pudsey, or 'Putsey' as the locals insist on calling it, the most recent being Pudsey Bear. This yellow teddy bear, complete with bandage, is the mascot of the BBC's Children in Need appeal and was adopted after work by the local hospital.

In Denby Dale, on the edge of Wakefield, the inhabitants celebrated the repeal of the protectionist Corn Laws in 1846 by baking one of their notorious giant pies. In Pudsey, 20 women mill workers produced a steamed fruit pudding; it took three days to cook.

There must be something in the water in Pudsey – something England's cricketers ought to have bottled to take on tour with them – for two of Yorkshire's greatest ever players, Herbert Sutcliffe and Sir Len Hutton, were born in the town. The latter played for the White Rose County for the whole of his career, scoring a century in his first Test against the old foe, Australia, in 1938. In the same series he scored 364 at the Oval and made 129 centuries in his first class career.

The **church of St Laurence** was built in 1821, just one of hundreds built by the Church of England in a bid to keep pace with the growth of industrial towns in the north and Midlands. Its most attractive feature is the ribbed ceiling.

QUEENSBURY [Bradford]

SE0929: 3 miles (5km) N of Halifax

Perched above Bradford on the 1100ft contour, Queensbury was a woollen manufacturing town. Locals also once worked in neighbouring coal mines. Today much of the industry has gone, but it remains a lively community. As in most other towns where wool was once spun and woven, look carefully beside some older buildings for a small hole bored in a vertical stone post. This is a 'wuzzing' hole in which a stick holding a net of washed yarn would be placed. Holding the other end, the weaver would then spin the net around the stick, forcing the water out – a Georgian version of the salad spinner!

The **church of the Holy Trinity** is another 1840s building erected to help the growing urban population keep the faith. It has an interesting double archway leading into the nave and the stained glass is worth a look.

RASTRICK [Calderdale]

SE1321: 3 miles (5km) SE of Halifax

Standing on the southern bank of the River Calder, Rastrick is perhaps best known in the eyes of many as one half of the famous Brighouse and Rastrick Brass

Band; needless to say, there is far more to the town than that. Historians believe there was a Roman settlement on the site, and that the road the invaders built between Chester and York went this way. What is certain is that it was occupied by Anglo-Saxon times because a carved **stone cross** base stands in the churchyard of **St Matthew's**. The church itself, probably standing on the site of an earlier one, is impressive. It was built at the end of the 18th century of finely honed ashlar blocks.

Many buildings date from the early and mid-Victorian period, when the town was growing as both a textile centre and one involved in light engineering and metalworking. One firm that survives has the distinction of being the second largest producer of metal coat-hangers in the world. Just remember that next time you go to the dry cleaners!

A famous former resident, or more accurately steward of **Firsby Hall** close by, was Richard Oastler (1789-1861). Known as the 'Factory King' he campaigned against slavery and the employment of children in factories – much the same thing really. He advocated a 10-hour factory working day, which led to the 10 Hours Act of 1847. For his pains, he was dismissed by his employer and spent four years in the Fleet Prison, for debt.

RIDDLESDEN [Bradford]

SE0741: 1 mile (2km) NE of Keighley

This settlement, which grew up on the edge of Keighley in the 19th century, enjoyed the familiar selection of West Riding industries and benefited from the Leeds and Liverpool Canal which cut through it. These days though, visitors come not to see the village itself but its treasure: **East Riddlesden Hall**. This important house is now in the care of the National Trust after a period during the 1930s when there were fears it would fall into dereliction. Its fate hung in the balance: demolition or to be dismantled and transported stone by stone to the USA. Thankfully, neither happened and it was bought by benefactors who saved it for the nation.

Built in 1642 by a wealthy Halifax clothier, James Murgatroyd, the building we see now was constructed on a medieval residence, nothing of which remains. Gabled and with stone mullions it boasts a marvellous rose window. Inside, the original central hall is magnificent and the building comes complete with period fireplaces and original oak panelling. Although the house was largely empty of furniture when the Trust took it over, it now brims over with a wonderful collection of items, most of them Yorkshire in origin or pedigree.

Outside there is more evidence of the great age of East Riddlesden, which experts reckon has a history dating to a century before the Conquest as the site of a Saxon manor house. The medieval tithe barn, or **Great Barn,** deserves its title and is a massive timber construction. Over the centuries, masonry has been added to create a structure considered the finest of its kind in the north of England. Nowadays, a collection of agricultural machines and vehicles is housed in the barn.

Entering the property today, the hall is seen across the unique and **ancient fish pond,** or 'Stagnum de Ridlesden' as it was called in the Compotus of Bolton Priory in 1320. Monks bred food fish, probably carp, in the pond, and in that year spent four shillings and threepence (21p) clearing the fish from here and elsewhere.

As if all this, together with pleasant period gardens, a shop and café weren't enough, East Riddlesden Hall must be one of the most haunted buildings in Yorkshire. At least five ghostly presences have been recorded trundling around its corridors and rooms, the most ghoulish being that of the Grey Lady. She is believed to be the ghost of a lady of the manor who was entertaining her lover when her husband inconveniently returned. Not a man of forgiving nature, he locked his wife in her room to starve, and had her boyfriend walled up nearby. The latter's face has been seen glowing in a wall, while the Lady herself roams the building. Legend has it that a skeleton, presumably of the lover, was once found behind a wall during repair work.

If that is a likely story, what of the one about the Scotsman who sought refuge there during a blizzard? Apparently a rich merchant, he was murdered by the master and his steward – the latter being

hanged at York in 1790 for his pains. The victim is reputed to be seen from time to time in a window above the front porch. There is also a White Lady in the grounds, most often seen by the pond; impressionable types reckon she represents a woman whose carriage ended up in the water one dark night. Look out too for the old cradle that is said to be rocked by an unseen hand every New Year's Eve. Anybody fancy spending the night here?

RIPPONDEN [Calderdale]

SE0420: 5 miles (8km) SW of Halifax

This is a fascinating Pennine town, sitting as it does high up and prone to snow and mist. Not surprisingly, it was wool that caused the place to develop, and the **Pennine Farm Museum** tells the story of hill farming in this unforgiving landscape. Housed in a farmhouse and barn close to the centre of Ripponden, the place is exhibited as it would have been in the 19th century when the family not only ran sheep on the moors but then turned their fleeces into cloth at their own loom.

The **church of St Bartholomew** was built in 1868 in the Early English style and its fine spire gives both it and the town added character. It is believed that a settlement grew up here thanks to a Roman ford over the River Ryburn. The current bridge dates from the first quarter of the 18th century. It was apparently built to replace an Elizabethan version washed away when the river flooded. The aptly named **Bridge Inn** next door is of a similar vintage.

The Roman connection with Ripponden adds interest for the visitor as it was undoubtedly on a route across the Pennines, from the salt and coal reserves of the north-west to the wool-rich parts of West and North Yorkshire. A few miles above Ripponden stands **Blackstone Edge**, a rocky ridge of millstone grit. In one direction is the sprawl of industrial Lancashire; in the other, wild and windy moorland. Cutting through it is a remarkably preserved packhorse route known to all as the **Roman Road**. Historians will argue forever about whether what we see today was tramped by the legions. They must have come this way, but it is likely it was widened and restored in later centuries. What is clear is that this 16ft-wide (5m) causeway with sturdy kerbs at each side was a busy highway from ancient times up to the middle of the 18th century. In the centre are large slabs with a deep groove running down the middle, apparently this would have been filled with turf to help pack animals get a purchase on the gradient.

RISHWORTH [Calderdale]

SE0318: 6 miles (10km) SW of Halifax

This small village close to the M62 must have been a lonely and isolated place a century ago. Nowadays it is a quiet place best known for **Rishworth School**, a private establishment with an excellent reputation. The buildings include a **chapel** built in 1725 which was the original school house, and an impressive, late Georgian, three-storey building constructed in 1825 to keep pace with the establishment's growing popularity.

ROBERTTOWN [Kirklees]

SE1922: 2 miles (3km) N of Mirfield

This village, surrounded though it is by other towns of similar background, had an extensive textile tradition until the industry collapsed after the Second World War. What is interesting, however, is that this was not so much a wool town as one in which cotton played a part. A Lancashire cotton magnate came here in the early part of the 19th century and built a five-storey spinning mill, providing much employment for several generations of local people. Contrary to general belief, cotton was not exclusively a Lancashire industry and wool a Yorkshire one. It is true that cotton spinning requires the damp climate typical of the area west of the Pennines (the moisture prevents the cotton thread from snapping during spinning), but Pennine Yorkshire has much the same weather. Between 1775 and 1850 in particular, a surprising number of cotton mills rubbed shoulders with woollen mills around Leeds, Halifax, Huddersfield and even Sheffield.

Robberttown has another place

in history, famed as the site of the biggest ever Chartist gathering in the 1840s. The Chartists were a working-class movement which began in 1837 and demanded the famous 'six points', including male suffrage, voting by secret ballot, abolition of the 'rotten boroughs' and payment for MPs. It grabbed the popular imagination, and led to many instances of public unrest, violence and peaceful protest. But those in power refused to relent and it died away after its final petition to Parliament was rejected in 1848.

chitecture, the tell-tale black and red quarry tiles give the game away. Beneath, or perhaps dumped in the churchyard, will be the original ancient flagstones – or even grave markers – which centuries of worship have worn smooth.

Buried here is the railway pioneer John Blenkinsop who built steam locomotives in the first decades of the 19th century. Forgotten by most, and wrongly eclipsed by Stephenson, he developed a line pulling coal on Hunslet Moor that is still operated by enthusiasts as the Middleton Railway.

ROTHWELL [Wakefield]

SE3428: 4½ miles (7km) SSE of Leeds

This town was once dominated by the coal mining industry and the countryside round about bears the scars. **The Church of the Holy Trinity** in Rothwell is a classic example, if ever one were needed, of the obsession the Victorians had with 'improving' ancient churches. This building is a fine example of the Perpendicular architecture popular in England from the later 14th century. The nave roof is marvellous, complete with fine bosses. So why then, did somebody come along in the 1870s and mess about so much with both the inside and outside?

It was seen as a great step forward at the time, and thousands of churches suffered in the same way. Take a look around your own local church. Even if you can't detect anything fundamental with the ar-

ROUNDHAY [Leeds]

SE3337: 1 mile (2km) NNE of Leeds

This might be considered a suburb of Leeds, but taking into account its proximity to the city centre, it is a remarkably peaceful and attractive place. For generations city dwellers have whiled away their free time in **Roundhay Park**. These 280 hectares (700 acres) of formal and informal gardens, complete with a range of Victorian buildings and other architectural pieces, form one of the 'green lungs' donated by wealthy benefactors to so many northern cities in the 19th century.

If the weather is too inclement to walk far in the park, don't hesitate to visit **Tropical World** across Prince's Avenue in the old **Coronation House.** The conservatory was built in 1911 next to the small but well-maintained Canal Gardens. This has to be the best value-for-money family attraction for miles. It is run by Leeds City Council and offers the largest collection of tropical plants outside Kew Gardens. But there is much more than plant life, including a magnificent butterfly house, ponds filled with hungry koi carp, aquaria containing all sorts of reptiles, amphibians and fish. Best of all is the nocturnal house. Here visitors can see creatures from the South American rainforest and a collection of Egyptian fruit bats swooping around in search of lunch. There is a shop and refreshments are available.

ROYSTON [Wakefield]

SE3611: 5½ miles (9km) SE of Wakefield

This proud town owes its existence to the coal mining industry, and its current state of melancholy to the destruction of the industry in the 1980s. While much of the architecture of note is Victorian, the **church of St John the Baptist** makes a detour here worthwhile. Perpendicular in character, it has a particularly tall tower with, unusually, an oriel window.

The roof to the nave has some excellent bosses and other carving – look out for the pelican and other animals. The monks of Monk Bretton Priory near Barnsley, who made their fortune from coal in medieval times, endowed it. A drive to this property is a 'must'. It is managed by English Heritage.

RYHILL [Wakefield]

SE3814: 2 miles (4km) W of Hemsworth

Before the Industrial Revolution this was no more than an agricultural hamlet, the name – logically enough – deriving from the hill on which rye was grown. The village we see now grew up in the 19th century when the vast coal reserves beneath its rye fields were so much in demand from the factory towns further west. There were pits all over this area, with first the **Barnsley Canal** and then two railway lines being constructed to cart the black gold away. That prosperity has gone now, but Ryhill is a welcoming place and attracts many commuters who work in Wakefield, Barnsley and beyond. Parts of the canal can still be walked and stretches offer refuge for wildfowl.

SALTAIRE [Bradford]

SE1438: 4½ miles (7km) NNE of Bradford

Some might think naming a town after yourself is the ultimate in self-adoration; even George Washington had the grace to die before his nation's capital took on his name. But while Sir Titus Salt might have been an egotist, he would never have admitted to a sin such as pride; his Nonconformist faith wouldn't have allowed it. But many of Sir Titus's faults can be forgiven, and his new town did take half of its name from the river that runs through it.

Sir Titus gave his textile workers some of the cleanest conditions in the country, together with their own specially designed homes. The first phase of **Saltaire** was opened in 1853, the great man's 50th birthday, and represented the success of a crusade which began in the previous decade. Then Lord Mayor of Bradford, his time in office coincided with one of the burgeoning city's all too common cholera epidemics. Hundreds died thanks to the almost total lack of proper sanitary arrangements and clean water. It was a blight that also ravaged other northern industrial towns such as Leeds and Manchester, but a sanitary report of 1844 condemned Bradford as one of the most squalid towns in Britain.

Appalled by what he saw, Sir Titus closed his four mills in Bradford and moved his operations, and his workers, to the pleasant, then rural, site close to the neighbouring town of **Shipley**. Served by first the Leeds and Liverpool Canal and then the railway, it was an ideal location for an experiment in industrial age social policy that had been started a few years earlier by Ackroyd, at **Copley** near Halifax.

Sir Titus engaged the Leeds architects Lockwood and Mawson (also responsible for Bradford Town Hall) and built a huge woollen **mill** complex, complete with a Venetian campanile-style chimney. Here his 3000 employees and 1200 looms produced 30,000 yards of cloth every day. The mill now houses a selection of shops and eating establishments, together with three galleries devoted to the work of Bradford-born artist **David Hockney**.

But a mill alone signifies nothing of Sir Titus's vision. He also built 775 houses close by, all with yards and in complete defiance of the 'back-to-back' types of dwellings common at the time. The streets, named after his wife Charlotte, his daughters, Queen Victoria and her family and the architects themselves, were built on a grid pattern looking down on the mill in the valley bottom. Determined to ensure his workers were healthy in both mind and body, the great Victorian philanthropist built a dispensary (later to become a small hospital with three wards), a park in which folk could take the air, shops and even wash-houses, complete with running water, wringing machines and drying rooms.

On **Victoria Square** are four magnificent **lions** sculpted by Thomas Milner and intended for Trafalgar Square in London, but considered too small. Legend has it that in the dark of night, the lions stir and walk down to the river to drink. Also on the square are two remarkable buildings. The first, the **Institute**, was used for the recreation and betterment of the workers. Sir Titus proclaimed it contained all the attractions of a public house, without any of its vices.

There was no alcohol – Sir Titus was a teetotaller and presumably decided that if he couldn't have a tipple nobody else could – or gambling, and not a pawn shop to be seen in the whole town. What the Institute did have though, was a library, a reading and conversation room, a concert hall, billiard room and science laboratory and gymnasium. Nowadays, the Institute is open to visitors, and houses the **Victorian Reed Organ Museum.** Here visitors can examine varying examples of an instrument which was once very popular, both here and in America – from where several examples come.

The building across the square was both a dining hall for the mill and a school for Saltaire's children. There were also almshouses, for those 'of good moral character', allotments, bathhouses and a boathouse down by the river. All these buildings survive, giving Saltaire a unique character and making the place an essential on any itinerary. The **Congregationalist church** also impresses. It was built in 1859 with a semicircular portico of six Corinthian columns. Not surprisingly, Sir Titus's faith refused to 'conform' to the strictures of the Church of England, much preferring a system of worship which allowed each community, or congregation, to go its own way.

The **Mausoleum** at the north-east end of the church holds the body of Sir Titus, who died in 1876. As a mark of respect, all the mills in Bradford stopped work on the day of his funeral. Inside the church there is a bust of Sir Titus, and there is a full-length statue of him in **Roberts Park** across the canal and river. In his hand he holds a piece of the cloth which made him

and Saltaire great, and there are representations of the alpaca and mohair-bearing animals that made his fortune. The park bears the name of the family who took over the mills and Saltaire's destiny after the Salt clan.

SANDAL [Wakefield]

SE3318: 1 mile (2km) S of Wakefield

More correctly known as Sandal Magna, this small village is now a suburb of Wakefield and boasts many fine and sought-after homes. The **church of St Helen** is an interesting cruciform shape, with the cross form further enhanced in the 19th century. Much of what we see today dates from the early 14th century and is in the Decorated style. There is a later Perpendicular chapel to the Waterton family, which held sway in the area right up to Victorian times. The screen is interesting with fine linenfold carving on the dado.

Most visitors these days come here to view **Sandal Castle.** Visible for miles around, the castle mound stands out on a flat plain not far from the River Calder and it is easy to see why the Normans decided to build one of their motte and bailey fortresses here. Originally it would have consisted of an earth mound surrounded by a wooden stockade and with the main building, again of wood, in the middle. By the 13th century it would have developed into a stone construction, but still maintaining a central keep with strong curtain walls. Apart from the clear motte and bailey outline and some tumbled masonry, there is little now to indicate its former glory. The castle's place in history came in 1460, at the height of the Wars of the Roses. The Battle of Wakefield alone is good reason to visit the site.

The background to the war is complicated, but naturally enough concerns the lust for power. The incompetent Henry VI was far from being the successful monarch some of the nobility expected, and he so angered his brilliant cousin, the Duke of York, that war was inevitable. When it came, Henry's wife Margaret, from the House of Lancaster, refused to allow her husband to lose his throne and organised resistance to York's rebellion. Early in 1460 the Yorkist army won a major victory at St Albans, but Margaret rallied and the two forces came into contact again on New Year's Eve that same year at Sandal.

York held the castle, but it was too small for his army, and his forces clashed with those of the Red Rose who had come from **Pontefract Castle**. In what was then heavily wooded country, Clifford, the Lancastrian commander, split his force. York sallied forth, surprised by the relatively small force his adversary had apparently deployed against him, and straight into a trap. When Clifford's men finally stood, York's force was well away from the castle on a slope now known as **Wakefield Green.** As battle commenced, the remaining Lancastrian forces poured out

of the woods from both flanks, surrounding and massacring York's men. The Duke of York himself was killed, either during the battle or immediately afterwards, and Queen Margaret ordered his head to be severed and displayed on a pike in Mickelgate Bar in York, wearing a paper crown. With it were the heads of Earls of Salisbury and Rutland. The latter, little more than a boy, was murdered by Clifford himself. As the boy knelt, begging for mercy, the bloodthirsty Clifford replied, 'Your father killed mine, so now I will kill you.' So much for chivalry.

Two centuries later the castle saw its final action when, held for the king, Cromwell's men besieged it. The commander tricked the Roundheads into holding a religious service and charged out and put them to flight. The victory did not last long, however, and when it fell it was destroyed, the same fate which befell its neighbour at Pontefract. Artefacts discovered during archaeological excavations of the site can be seen in **Wakefield Museum.**

SEACROFT [Leeds]
SE3135: 2 miles (3km) NE of Leeds

A suburb of Leeds, Seacroft was once a township in its own right. While some might consider it has lost its identity, swallowed up by the city, it has a pleasant village green. The **church of St James** was built in 1846 with an octagonal spire to give presence and character.

SCAMMONDEN WATER [Calderdale]

SE0516: 2½ miles (4km) SE of Ripponden

This remarkable **reservoir** provides water to the towns of Halifax and its neighbours, all of which are visible to the west. The dam wall is crossed by the **M62**, which raised a huge mound of earth to allow the road to cross a steep-sided valley. This highway is one of the most scenically interesting in the region. Opened by the Queen in 1971, the reservoir holds an incredible 1730 millions gallons.

While providing water for homes and industry is its purpose, the reservoir is also popular with water sports enthusiasts. Walkers use the paths around its shores for an excellent circular ramble. Above Scammonden is **Deanhead Reservoir,** built in 1836 to supply textile mills in the Colne Valley. The local **Deanhead Church** was first erected in 1615, but the current building is Victorian.

SCARCROFT [Leeds]

SE3541: 6 miles (9km) SW of Wetherby

This former agricultural village stands on the main A58 between Leeds and Wetherby. Its pleasant appearance and rural setting now attract folk working in the former city. Historians believe the Romans had a camp here, and there is certainly evidence that they built a road close to the current main highway. Buildings of interest include the **Scarcroft Water Mill,** built in 1810 to grind corn.

SCHOLES [Leeds]

SE3424: 5 miles (8km) E of Leeds

Another former agricultural village which now acts as a dormitory for commuters. Not that it is any worse for that. Who can blame those who choose to live in such a pleasant environment if their circumstances allow? The village didn't have a church until 1875, and the small one built then has been succeeded by another constructed in 1960. They stand in interesting contrast.

SHELF [Bradford]

SE1228: 4 miles (6km) SSW of Bradford

The agricultural character of this village remains, with two splendid farmhouses of the 17th century, **High Bentley** and **Lower Bentley,** bearing interesting features. **The church of St Michael** was built in 1850.

SHELLEY [Kirklees]

SE2011: 4½ miles (7km) NNE of Holmfirth

This is a traditional Pennine village overlooking the Holme Valley. In days gone by it was both a farming and a mining community (although little evidence of the latter remains today). There was also cottage-based woollen manufacture, as in so many villages in this area, and many of the houses date from the 17th and 18th centuries. One of the most interesting buildings is **Shelley Hall,** which dates from the 1600s and stands close to the church. Nearby is a pinfold, once a familiar sight in every agricultural village, but now extremely rare. A pinfold, the name is derived from an Old English word, was used to impound stray sheep or cattle; the owner usually having to pay a fee to get his beasts back.

residents gave rise to the twice-yearly Shepley Races. This event marked the handing out of the 'divi', or dividend bonus paid out by the village's most important shop, the co-op. Folk would dash down the road to get their pay-outs, and then presumably spend it just as quickly, hence the name.

SHEPLEY [Kirklees]

SE1909: 3 miles (5km) ENE of Holmfirth

Woe betide those who confuse this village and Shelley. Just a few miles and one consonant apart, they are entirely different places – in both size and character. Shepley is the larger, and at a lower altitude on either side of the main Huddersfield to Penistone Road. Its neighbour Shelley is 'oop on t'tops' to the north-east.

There were once four mills in the village, all producing fine woollen worsteds at such a rate that in the 19th century there were no fewer than 30 tailor's shops in a community of just over 1000 souls. Sadly, the shops have all gone now, together with most of the 20 sweet shops recorded by a local historian. But the **railway station** remains, providing transport on the Huddersfield to Penistone line, one of the most attractive in West Yorkshire with its numerous viaducts and the opportunities to look down from the line into other people's gardens.

Before the Second World War, Shepley was a thriving and busy community and the industry of its

SHIBDEN [Calderdale]

SE1025: 1 mile (2km) E of Halifax

Approach this pleasant village on the edge of Halifax and the odds on seeing a few sheep on the way will be poor for anybody who likes a bet. There have been sheep in this area for 1000 years, and while the last couple of centuries saw woollen manufacture expand enormously, the animal has always provided a livelihood in this area. Hence, therefore, the name Shibden as a derivation from the Nordic 'Scepedene', or 'Sheep Vale'.

The wealth wool brought led to the construction of a number of grand farmhouses, several of which still survive on the inhospitable moorland above the village. Scout Hall, built in 1680, is one of the finest such mansions, with local historians relishing the story of its first owner. A dilettante and boozer of heroic proportions, his orgies, drinking parties and other outrages came to a permanent halt when he leapt from the building wearing a pair of ineffective wings.

The biggest attraction for visitors

is **Shibden Hall,** now open to the public and one of the finest examples in the region of 15th-century parochial architecture. The black and white timber facade has twin gables and was built by the Otes family in the 1420s.What makes it particularly interesting is that while the house has developed, grown, contracted and altered over the centuries, evidence of each period still exists. There is a fine collection of furniture and household objects from the 17th and 18th centuries.

Also worth a visit is the **West Yorkshire Folk Museum** contained in the 17th-century barn. Here is an important collection of old agricultural machinery and artefacts, together with a large variety of horse-drawn vehicles, from hearses to fire engines, farm carts to smart coaches.

Outside, the cobbled courtyard is arranged as an early 19th-century village where the visitor can look at the apothecary's shop or try the pub games of the period, look inside an estate worker's cottage and admire the skills which went into a range of traditional crafts.

Shibden Hall stands in the grounds of **Shibden Park**, a 36-hectare (90-acre) expanse of rolling countryside with ample space for picnics and walking, There is also an orienteering course, boating lake, children's play area and cafe.

SHIPLEY [Bradford]

SE1537: 3 miles (5km) NNW of Bradford

A stone's throw from Saltaire, Shipley is not caught in the same time warp and continues to grow and develop as a busy town with things to do. Having said that, the visitor will find the town's historical features an interesting companion to those down the road, ensuring this fascinating part of Airedale receives at least a day of your time.

In Shipley itself is the **church of St Paul,** built in 1823 when manufacturing industry saw the local population soar. Built in the Perpendicular style, as was fashionable at the time, the church has a pleasant stained-glass picture in the east window. Motorcycle fans will nostalgically recall that the famous builder Alfred Angus Scott built his first bike in Shipley in 1906. The Scott Trial, run in the Yorkshire Dales each October for moto-cross exponents, still bears his name.

Near to the railway station, on Leeds Road, is Windmill Manor, home to a fascinating exhibition for cat lovers. **'Furever Feline'** is lots of fun, especially for children, with powered models and tableaux.

The **Leeds and Liverpool Canal,** that seminal waterway in the history of the region's industrial development, cuts through the Aire Valley at Shipley. This section, linking the Aire and Calder basins, was built in the 1770s, but it was well into the next century when the whole trans-Pennine route was completed. Then it brought fuel, food and minerals to Shipley, Bingley, Bradford and other growing towns, taking away their textiles and other heavy goods. Nowadays it is possible to walk the canal towpath, or, from **Shipley Wharf**, take a narrow boat up the canal, through Saltaire and on to Bingley. On the way, passengers can alight at Saltaire and visit the fascinating model town, or, on the other side of the valley, explore **Shipley Glen**. This justly popular beauty spot has been popular with the people of Bradford and its surrounding towns for generations. At the bottom of the Glen, a feature called the **Devil's punchbowl** was the scene of much interest. A number of people claimed to see a large grey bird with a long beak and swore blind it was a pterodactyl. Those familiar with the appearance of the grey heron, a far more common species in these parts, were determined it was not one of them, and lovers of mysteries happily claim the sighting as some sort of X-Files style visitation. Keep your eyes peeled!

In 1895 a unique cable-powered **tramway** was built linking the Glen with pleasure gardens at the top of the hill. It has now been restored and is open to visitors from Easter onwards.

From here visitors are recommended to take a look at the **Bracken Hill Countryside Centre** and learn a little about the wildlife and ecology of the area.

SLAITHWAITE [Kirklees]

SE0714: 4½ miles (7km) SW of Huddersfield

The best way to visit Slaithwaite, or 'Slawit' as it should be properly pronounced, is not by car on the Huddersfield road, but on foot. There was a time when it would have been possible to travel here by water, on the **Huddersfield Narrow Canal**, but the way between here and Huddersfield itself has been filled in at several spots for many years. As a result, the favoured route has to be via the canal towpath, either from Huddersfield, or from Marsden and **Tunnel End**. The canal linked Manchester with West Yorkshire via the remarkable Standedge Tunnel, and in so doing brought the Industrial Revolution to Slaithwaite.

Prior to the start of the 19th century, the town was much the same as any other in the Calder valley. Families would farm sheep, raise a few vegetables, then weave or spin in their three-storey weaver's cottages. There are still plenty of these to be seen both in the town and along the canal on either side. In addition, there are numerous small 'manufactories' that harnessed the water from the many streams which run down the valley. Soon, inevitably, these were replaced by much bigger mills, one or two of which still survive, albeit in different use.

The town itself once had its own 'dock' for the loading and unloading of heavy goods, including stone which was quarried nearby. A goodly percentage of this was taken by narrow boat under the Pennines and into Lancashire for that county's cotton mills and public buildings. Most of the buildings in the town are Victorian, but especially interesting is the ensemble of buildings which includes the **church of St James,** built in 1789, complete with Venetian window and west tower. Nearby is the late 16th-century **Manor House,** complete with mullioned windows. Not far away stands the **Old Free School**, now a funeral director's premises, which used to provide education for the town's children. Hereabouts too is the 'public lock-up', complete with four cells where local ne'er do wells could cool their heels after a night on the tiles.

Customers of the lock-up might have been the smugglers who used to hide their contraband in the canal, away from the eyes of the customs men. Surprised one night as they attempted to recover their submerged cache of goodies, they claimed to be attempting to rake the moon from the water. Whether they got away with it or not is unknown, but they became known at 'the Slawit moonrakers' and a festival commemorating the event is held every February. One of Slaithewaite's best-known residents was the violinist and song writer Haydn Wood (1882-1959). The appropriately named Haydn composed a large amount of work, including the First World War anthem, 'Roses of Picardy'.

SOUTH ELMSALL [Wakefield]
SE4710: 3 miles (5km) ESE of Hemsworth
A town which not many years ago was booming, South Elmsall is an-

other victim of the collapse of the coal mining industry in the 1980s. Where once there were four or five pits within walking distance, now there are none – an event that has had a devastating impact on the local economy. There is a regular **market** here, and local non-league soccer team Frickley Athletic pulls in decent crowds.

SOUTH KIRKBY [Wakefield]
SE4510: 2 miles (3km) SE of Hemsworth
Just up the road from South Elmsall, this village also grew up around mining, and suffered the consequences of its demise. The **church of All Saints** is impressive and Perpendicular in style. Especially interesting is the ornate south porch, which displays shields of local families. Inside there are some impressive arches and a stone tablet to John Wentworth made in 1720 and signed by the acclaimed Flemish sculptor Michael Rysbrack. His work includes the monument to Sir Isaac Newton that stands in Westminster Abbey. Near the town, standing on a hill, is an **Iron Age encampment,** with substantial defensive mounds still visible.

The local school, **Minsthorpe High School**, is the alma mater of playwright John Godber whose *Bouncers, Up and Under* and other social tragi-comedies say more than any academic study about the humour and tribulations of industrial West Yorkshire at the end of the 20th century.

SOWERBY [Calderdale]

SE0423: 1mile (3km) SW of Sowerby Bridge

Sitting between the valleys of the Rivers Ryburn and Calder, this small village looks down on its larger namesake by the bridge over the latter waterway. It might not have as much to say for itself, but the church of St Peter, built in 1766, is most impressive and grand in the classical style, with both a sundial and clock on the tower. Also here is a statue to local boy made good John Tillotson. Despite marrying a niece of Oliver Cromwell, he became chaplain to King Charles II and later Archbishop of Canterbury.

SOWERBY BRIDGE [Calderdale]

SE0625: 5 miles (8km) SSE of Halifax

If ever an example were needed of a town 'pulling itself up by its bootstraps', this is it. For two centuries Sowerby Bridge was a hive of industrial activity, with woollen textile production taking pride of place and providing thousands of jobs. But the industry, as elsewhere in the county, had no chance when competing with cheap foreign imports, and as the factories closed their gates for the last time the town was on its uppers. Thanks, however, to some remarkable energy and enthusiasm, Sowerby Bridge is reviving itself on leisure and tourism, and making the most of its industrial heritage.

The town is in a unique position: sited in the Calder Gap, it was on an ancient route across the Pennines, linking Yorkshire with Lancashire. The bridge, dating from the 17th century although greatly altered over the centuries, was the traditional crossing point of the River Calder for the long packhorse trains that lumbered through these hills. Nearby is the River Ryburn, another waterway that helped boost the town's textile legacy.

Historians are able to trace woollen goods production here to water-driven mills of the 14th century, and while they are not visible any more we can see Greenups Mill, built in 1792. This was the first integrated woollen mill in Yorkshire, bringing all the production stages under one roof and tolling the death knell on the 'domestic system' of textile production. Standing beside the Calder, the mill, which once had 100 looms, has been converted to residential use. Nearby stood Longbottoms Mill, which when built in 1770 used manual power. A stone's throw away is Carlton Mill, built in 1850 and powered by steam engines. The history of the site provides a fascinating look at the development of the industry that helped clothe the Empire.

Sowerby Bridge's importance as a junction of the Calder and Hebble Navigation, built in 1770, and the Rochdale Canal (1804), cannot be overestimated. It was a crossroads of commerce and industry, a powerhouse where peace

The Leeds-Liverpool Canal at Sowerby Bridge

and tranquillity are now enjoyed by locals and visitors alike. The Rochdale Canal, the most successful trans-Pennine waterway, has the deepest lock in the country, **Lock 3**, just off Tuel Lane, an amazing 30ft drop. Not far away is the **wharf**, now a marina, where produce would be transhipped between canals (infuriatingly the two waterways had locks of different lengths and needed different types of vessels to navigate them). Surrounding the Wharf are warehouses dating back to the end of the 18th century, now converted to craft and art galleries.

Perhaps it is not surprising that in the early 19th century the townspeople decided their small Tudor church needed replacing and so built **Christ Church** in 1821. The communion table dating back to the earlier Old Brigg Chapel of 1526 stands inside.

The ancient custom of rush-bearing is still celebrated here, with a procession in September which takes in the neighbouring village of Sowerby.

STANBURY [Bradford]

SE0037: 1 mile (2km) W of Haworth

If you were on the lookout for a 'typical' Pennine village, this might be it. Standing on the hillside, with the infant River Worth flowing down the nearby valley, its largely 18th- and 19th-century houses show ample of evidence of the days when nearly every home had its own spinning wheel or handloom – or both. Fans of the Brontës will feel at home here, even if it is a century and a half since the talented trio trod these hills.

Experts on their work reckon this

immediate area features again and again in the books, with the ruin of **Top Withens** falling within Stanbury's parish boundaries. This tumbledown farmhouse of soot-blackened gritstone is said by most to be Emily's model for Wuthering Heights. Nearby is Ponden Hall, identified as Thushcross Grange in the same book. A few hundred metres away is the **Pennine Way**, the demanding route from Edale in Derbyshire to Kirk Yeatholm just over the Scottish border. Take care when walking in this area, as it is not only the treacherous moorland mists that can put you to fright. The suspicious claim Emily's ghost is sometimes seen walking the old packhorse route between Stanbury and Top Withens, while others have seen her spirit near the so-called **Brontë Falls** nearby. Another Brontë connection is the wooden pulpit in the **church**, a remnant of the three-level pulpit that stood in the old church at nearby Haworth that would have been used many times by the sisters' father.

Ponden Mill, built in 1791, is a good example of a cotton mill that later went over to worsted spinning as production of the fine woollen cloth increased in this part of the county. The mill still stands and now operates as a mill shop. Contrastingly, the village was also the home of Timmy Feather, reputed to be the West Riding's last handloom weaver. His machine is on display in **Cliffe Castle Museum** in Keighley.

STANLEY [Wakefield]

SE3424: 1 mile (2km) NE of Wakefield

It is easy to understand why considerable evidence of ancient occupation and trading activity has been found in this area. A natural fording point on the River Calder, Roman legions will have crossed here two millennia ago, almost certainly assisted by local ferrymen. It is a tradition that carried on for centuries, to the extent that the town is still known by some as Stanley Ferry.

The Industrial Revolution brought coal miners to the area, the result of their labours being floated away on the Aire and Calder Navigation which flows close by. Here, at the point of the old ferry, the river was crossed by an **aqueduct** in 1839. Although not in use, it can still be seen today.

The **church of St Peter** was built in the 1820s, a so-called 'Waterloo' church, but was burned down in 1911. The replacement, by the much-admired W.D. Caroe, is a remarkable structure with two thin towers on the west front. The wide, bright and airy interior is a lovely sight. Beneath, the large crypt from the Georgian church survives.

STEETON [Bradford]

SE0344: 3 miles (5km) NW of Keighley

Although set in the heart of the largely industrialised Aire Valley, Steeton's character says agriculture rather than industry. Two important 17th-century buildings, named imaginatively **High Hall** and **Low Hall**, are traditional Yorkshire manor houses of the type and design owned by wealthy yeoman farmers.

In the village, **the parish church of St Stephen** is of late Victorian date; prior to that locals went to Kildwick a few miles away, further evidence of how the township's growth was late in coming.

SWILLINGTON [Leeds]

SE3830: 5½ miles (9km) SSE of Leeds

start = An Airedale village which saw its boom years in the 19th century, Swillington's **church of St Mary** displays ample evidence of a Victorian architect's determination to improve on 14th-century perfection. The original church, in Decorated and Perpendicular styles, had a tower built in the 1400s, no doubt matching perfectly the Tadcaster honey-coloured stone of the rest of the structure. In the 1880s this was replaced by a 'modern' one in a stone that has long been blackened by air pollution. The church is, nonetheless, worth a visit and contains an interesting carved oak effigy.

A couple of miles away, along the A642 in the direction of Oulton, is the complex of subsidence flashes and small lakes making up the nature reserve of **New Swillington Ings.** Also known as Astley Lakes, this area is a major attraction to both migrating birds looking for a place to roost, and breeding birds attracted by a series of open water refuges along the River Aire. This reserve, managed by the local bird group, is especially interesting from March to June, and from August until October, when any number of interesting migrants might pop up. There is both parking and a hide for birdwatchers.

TEMPLE NEWSAM [Leeds]

SE3532: 4 miles (6km) E of Leeds

This gem is, remarkably, Europe's largest urban park, and a welcome presence on the edge of a bustling city such as Leeds. There has been a building on the site for centuries and the name supports historical belief that the estate was owned by the Knights Templars at the height of their power in the 13th century.

Nothing is left visible of that time, but the magnificent building which now bears the name has been described – without irony – as the Hampton Court of the North. Like its Thameside relative, its origins lie in the first quarter of the 16th century. It was built by Thomas, Lord Darcy, a soldier and statesman who fought for his country in Spain and France. He fell from favour when he spoke out against Henry VIII's divorce of Catherine of Aragon. Opposing the Dissolution of the Monasteries cost him his head in 1537.

The buildings were altered a century later, but the red brick and stone decoration form the mansion's predominantly Jacobean character. Alterations in keeping with the original design were made later, but little remains inside to show the original nature of the structure.

Nonetheless, it takes little imagination, standing outside, to imagine Henry Stewart, better known by his title, Lord Darnley, striding up the steps of his birthplace. Darnley, of course, was the scheming, and ultimately schemed against, second husband of Mary, Queen of Scots. The pair seemed to have sealed a love match and there seems little doubt he was responsible for murdering his wife's private secretary, David Rizzio, at Holyrood House in 1566. Differences over religion and the lure of wealth and power drove a wedge between Mary and Darnley, however, despite the fact that the pair had a son, later to become James I of England and 6th of Scotland. When Darnley caught smallpox his regal wife appeared to soften and nursed him for days at Edinburgh. All seems to have been a ruse, however, because in February 1567 she went to a dinner and returned to find that the house had been blown up and Darnley lying dead in the garden. The main conspirator was the Earl of Bothwell, who both got away with the crime and soon after married the Queen.

Not surprising then that Temple Newsam is supposed to have at least three ghosts, including a Templar Knight, a small child and, in the Long Gallery, a ghostly fog which transforms itself into various spectral forms. Take a look for yourself, the house is now a **museum** containing Leeds City Council's excellent collection of paintings, ceramics and furniture.

The **gardens and grounds**, ideal for a summer afternoon's stroll, were modelled by 'Capability' Brown in the 18th century and include lakes, terraces and lovely woodland walks. Another attraction, especially for children, is the **home farm**. It is based around the old stable blocks and boasts a fascinating collection of rare domestic animals.

THORNHILL [Kirklees]
SE2518: 2 miles (3km) S of Dewsbury

This small settlement has more to say about Tudor times than the industrial fervour which came to the area four centuries later. Thornhill was the home of the Savile family, a dynasty of landowners, statesmen and protectors of religious tolerance who had their 16th-century home, now a ruin, across the road from **St Michael and All Angels Church**.

Although the nave was rebuilt in the 19th century, much of what is left, including the tower, is 15th century – and what a marvellous structure it is. After feasting one's eyes on the exterior, the interior demonstrates why so many come to marvel. There is an important collection of **Anglo-Saxon crosses**, three marked with ancient runes, and another bearing the name 'Osbert'. Could this have been the stone that stood over the grave of King Osbert, who was killed by the Danes at York in 867?

Later monuments to great men and women include remarkable sculpture in the **Savile Chapel** of 1477 and elsewhere in the church, including one in alabaster and a knight in mail and another in armour. Another rarity is an oak 'tomb chest' from the 16th century.

More important, perhaps, than all the above is the late medieval **stained glass**, again much of it in the Savile Chapel, which has four lovely windows. But the most noteworthy of all must be the magnificent east window in the design of a Jesse Tree and tracing the genealogy of Christ.

In the last 200 years Thornhill, along with neighbouring towns and villages, has been embraced by heavy industry, particularly coal mining. Perhaps inevitably, it has had its share of tragedy. The worst occurred in 1893 at Combs Pit when an underground gas explosion killed 139 men and boys – just seven surviving out of the whole shift. Another 11 men died at the same mine just after the Second World War.

THORNTON [Bradford]

SE1032: 4 miles (6km) W of Bradford

Although now, essentially, a part of the city of Bradford, Thornton should be seen in the context of the beginning of the 19th century. Then it was a small village surrounded by hills and very much a community in its own right. It was here, and to the old **church of St James**, that Patrick Brontë came as curate in 1816. Over the next four years his wife Maria Branwell gave birth to a trio of remarkable sisters, and their brother Branwell, in a little house on **Market Street**. The house can still be seen, and many Brontë followers make a pilgrimage to Thornton before continuing to Haworth and the parsonage with which they are most associated.

While the church in which Patrick Brontë led worship in is now in ruins, a Victorian replacement, of the same name, stands nearby. It has a fine Morris window, and the font, dated 1687, in which the literary sisters were baptised.

THURSTONLAND [Kirklees]

SE1610: 2 miles (3km) NE of Holmfirth

This isolated village stands above the Holme Valley and was once a booming hill farming community. Nowadays, many of the farm buildings have been turned into private homes, but some still eke a living from the land, running sheep on the moors. Across the valley, on **Harden Moors**, visitors in June can witness one of the last – and finest – sheep dog trials in Yorkshire (wrap up warm – it is always bitterly cold, but worth it for the experience).

Fans of Compo and his friends in the television series 'Last of the Summer Wine' will recognise some of the buildings and country around Thurstonland.

TODMORDEN [Calderdale]

SD9324: 6 miles (10km) SW of Hebden Bridge

What a grand place Todmorden is. 'Tod', as it is known to anybody born within a 25-mile radius, once straddled the boundary between Yorkshire and Lancashire and owes as much to the cotton production of the Red Rose county as to the woollen trade of the White. Until the middle of the 20th century the county boundary passed through the middle of the town, half of the 1870 town hall standing in Lancashire, half in Yorkshire; a subject of much ribaldry during political debates. Your whole cultural future depended on the side of the boundary line on which one was born – were you a 'Lanc' or a 'Tyke'?

The schizophrenic nature of the town is displayed on the front of the **town hall**, likened by Pevsner to that of Birmingham, where the frieze shows bales of cotton on the western side and wool on the eastern. Nearby is the fine early 17th-century **Old Hall**, once dubbed the largest sub-post office in England, but now put to other use.

While there may have always been a settlement at this natural gap through the Pennines, it was the coming of the canals, followed later by a road, which transformed what would have been a tiny farming community into one of the most important towns in this part of West Yorkshire. The **Rochdale Canal** was originally surveyed by the great James Brindley, the illiterate designer of the seminal Bridgewater Canal, but not completed until 1804. By this date canal building was in decline, but the Rochdale was a winner, despite the troublesome terrain, and successfully linked the great trading city of

Manchester with the cotton powerhouse of Rochdale. It then continued over the 'tops' to Hebden Bridge and the Calder and Hebble Navigation

In **Todmorden Park,** home of the regionally famous 'Tod Show', stands a statue to 'Honest John' Fielden. One of the true Victorian philanthropists, he was both the MP and owner of the town's most important textile company, yet he spent his life campaigning for improvements to the conditions of factory workers. A colleague of Lord Shaftesbury, he helped bring in the 'Ten Hours Bill' and is buried in the Unitarian cemetery.

Another of the town's famous sons was the great scientist Sir John Cockcroft, who won the Nobel Prize for Physics in 1951 and is credited with being the first man to split the atom.

TONG [Bradford]

SE2130: 4 miles (6km) SE of Bradford

Although but a stone's throw from the centre of Bradford, this attractive village still retains a rural charm which makes it popular with those who have to earn their living in the city proper. Tong takes its character from Sir George Tempest, resident at **Tong Hall** in the early 1700s. This gentleman was responsible for the complete remodelling of **St James's Church** in 1727, incorporating much earlier bits and pieces from its predecessor. It is of particular importance for the 18th-century fittings, including a three-storey pulpit and fine high, and low, box pews. In order to ensure nobody was in doubt about who was top dog in Tong, the Tempest family pew has its own fireplace.

The hall was built in 1702 by the same Sir George and is recorded as the only important brick building of the 18th century now standing in the Bradford area. It comes complete with perfectly balanced bays and carving in the style of Grinling Gibbons adorns the walls.

TUNNEL END [Kirklees]

SE0412: 1 mile (2km) W of Marsden

This remote and severe place, high up on the very rise of the Pennines, is cold and forbidding for most of the year. Naturally enough, therefore, it is the home of what must be one of the most important examples of 'industrial archaeology' in the country – and it is little known to most.

The **Standedge Tunnel** (Standedge is a corruption of 'Stanage' or 'edge of stones') is one of the remarkable achievements of a period when man appeared to fear nothing and to see everything as a challenge to his ingenuity and self-belief.

Begun in 1798, it took 12 years to complete and stretches three miles, 135 yards (5km) from Tunnel End west of Marsden, under Standedge Moor to emerge near Diggle in Lancashire. The tunnel was ventilated by a shaft 645ft deep, but the air inside must have been foul and took 'liggers' – boat-

men lying on their back and pushing barges through with their legs on the tunnel walls – four hours to make the journey.

The journey, on the **Huddersfield Narrow Canal**, linked Huddersfield with Ashton-under-Lyne. Although huge sums were soaked up by the enterprise it hardly made a profit and soon gave way to rail. In 1845 the first of three railway tunnels was dug under Standedge, using the canal tunnel next door to take the spoil away, and thus signing the waterway's death warrant. At completion in 1848 it was the longest railway tunnel in the world.

It is possible to follow a trail over the moor along the line of the tunnel and a **visitor centre** at Tunnel End provides an interesting introduction to this fascinating area. Turn east, and a well-restored footpath walk follows the Narrow Canal back into the centre of Huddersfield.

UNDERCLIFFE [Bradford]

SE1734: 1 mile (2km) NNE of Bradford

This cemetery on the edge of Bradford city centre is an absolute gem. Their mills might have gone, their homes might be occupied by solicitors, architects and bed and breakfast hotels, but if you were ever in doubt about what made the woollen kings of Bradford tick, it is here.

If urban architecture demanded conservatism from its benefactors, and the reserved lines and understated elegance of many a northern town's public buildings show that more than likely it did, then it was not a rule which applied to the afterlife. A stroll around **Undercliffe Cemetery** is more about the Victorians' way of life than of death – but in those days the latter was always waiting around the corner.

What is waiting around the corner here, as the visitor drives up New Otley Road and on to Undercliffe Lane, is an astonishing necropolis devoted to Bradford's great and good – and the city's not very great and on occasion not very good either. Opened in 1854, this 10.5-hectare (26-acre) site looks down on the city below, the city which made many who lie here very rich indeed. Apparently, the better the view, the pricier the plot – presumably more important for the living who visited the place than those beneath their feet! And plenty were prepared to pay the price. There is row after row of the most grandiose obelisks, crosses, spires and pinnacles imaginable, the kind of display more familiar in Latin America than West Yorkshire.

Cemetery visiting, not a mass-market pastime these days, was popular a century ago and Undercliffe's founders made clear their aim in their first handbook of rules: 'They desire to throw the cemetery open to the public as much as possible. So long as propriety of behaviour is observed, none will be excluded from the grounds who desire to avail themselves thereof, either as a place of relaxation or for contemplative retirement.'

It is clear that as far as the fabulously rich **Illingworths** were concerned, they considered themselves as first among equals. Their mausoleum, a recreation of an Egyptian Temple with sphinxes sitting outside the entrance to the vault, would look more at home in Disneyland than Bradford; what a scandal it must have caused in those strait-laced times. All around are other monstrosities, each trying to outdo their neighbours in size and expense.

Take a walk around, not forgetting the graves of the less well-off Bradfordians on a history tour of this great city's Victorian past. You will never consider our current culture vulgar again.

UPPERTHONG [Kirklees]

SE1308: 1 mile (2km) W of Holmfirth

What a place this must have been when, before mechanisation proper took woollen textile production down into the Holme Valley, many families made their living spinning and weaving their textiles in their homes for sale in nearby cloth halls.

Upperthong – the name betrays its Viking founders, 'thing' being the Nordic name for a place where armed men would congregate – is on the 1000ft contour and suffers all the weather the Pennines can throw at it. The houses in the centre of the village, now a conservation area, include a number of three-storey buildings from the

18th century and before. The top storey, and this whole area is a treasure house of such homes, would have been one long room where handlooms operated; some have a large doorway and stairs at the back, down which the finished product would be carried.

In the moorland hills beyond the town are numerous farmsteads of the 'laithe-house' design. Constructed as one rectangular building, it would be split down the middle: a traditional farmhouse on one side, a barn on the other. Look for the arched main barn door, designed to take a fully loaded hay cart. Built of local gritstone, these farmhouses represented the beginning of the woollen textile trade. It was here that sheep were bred, raised and shorn to provide the raw material that made West Yorkshire rich.

WAKEFIELD [Wakefield]
SE3320: 9 miles (15km) SSE of Leeds

This is the county town of both the old West Riding of Yorkshire, and the now defunct West Yorkshire County Council which followed it in the 1970s. Smaller than Leeds or Bradford, these latter two were mere villages in comparison to Wakefield prior to the beginning of the 18th century.

Before then, Wakefield was a centre for cloth marketing, having its own cloth hall, or 'piece hall', to which local people would bring quantities of rough textile cloth made in their own homes. The cottage manufacture of woollen and cotton cloth involved whole families, who spun yarn and then wove it on looms on the top floor of their homes. When complete, the material would be brought to a centre such as Wakefield and traded with merchants who had the products finished elsewhere. Sitting above the River Calder, Wakefield was a centre of such trade from the time of the Conquest; by the Middle Ages it justly deserved its role as the county town.

The best evidence of the town's importance (it only became a city at the end of the 19th century) can be seen in the size and grandeur of the **cathedral church of All Saints.** The exterior of the building is entirely Perpendicular, having been built, in most part, between the middle of the 14th century and the middle of the next. Inside, a host of different influences come into play, but the whole is a splendid structure – a truly grand parish church of the first division. The west tower is a prominent structure and, because the church was built on a slight rise, can be seen from miles away. On top is a spire built in 1420 and reaching a height of 247ft (75m), making it the highest in the whole of Yorkshire.

The great Victorian church architect Sir Gilbert Scott restored the spire and much of the exterior of the building over 16 years from 1858. Inside, there are a number of features dating back to the mid-12th century, including some Norman piers, plus more from the 1200s. There are some interesting furnishings in the cathedral, in-

The cathedral, Wakefield

The cathedral stands at a junction of streets whose names bear witness to the city's antiquity: Westgate, Northgate and Kirkgate – the word 'gate', or 'gard' being Norse for 'street'. The Viking city of York has more: Coppergate, Micklegate and Stonegate. Wakefield's **Westgate**, leading from the cathedral down to the **railway station** of the same name, is full of character and interest, so much so that it has been turned into a local Conservation Area. In the Middle Ages Westgate, along with the other two 'gates', was barred at 8pm to prevent unruly behaviour or worse entering the inner area of the town. The importance of Wakefield as a textile trading centre saw Westgate adorned with a number of grand merchant's buildings and banks to service them; many of those built in the 18th and 19th centuries survive.

Breaking off at right angles to Westgate are a number of narrow streets which would have originally been areas for stabling or with small allotment gardens. Later, they would house craftsmen and their workshops, while **Cheapside** boasts the longest continuous street of woolstapler's

cluding a font of 1661 and a beautifully carved rood screen dating back to 1635. A three-decker pulpit of 1708 is interesting and the misericords in the chancel are particularly amusing: look out for a juggler with his head between his legs, a pelican and a Tudor rose. Most of the glass is Victorian, the work of the finest craftsman of his age, C.E. Kempe. **Monuments** include one of 1714 to Sir Lyon Pilkington, from a distant branch of the Lancastrian glass family, whose lands included the estate at **Newmillerdam**.

warehouses in England. **Barstow's Yard**, where Westgate becomes Silver Street, still has the original cobbles brought to surface the street from the nearby River Calder. At the bottom of Westgate, beneath the railway viaduct, look out for the grand doorway that was the original entrance to the station.

North-west of the cathedral runs **Wood Street**, which contains the city's most important 19th-century public buildings. The first of them was built in 1820 and is called the Mechanic's Institution on the frieze, but was also known as the Institute of Literature and Science. These public rooms would have been used for readings, debates on the science and literature of the time, and other intellectual pastimes such as musical recitals. Nowadays it houses **Wakefield Museum**, which takes a detailed look at the development of Wakefield from the earliest times and holds a collection of finds from both **Sandal Castle** and Roman **Castleford**. Most remarkable of all must be the collection of novelties, curios, natural history specimens and other items collected during a lifetime of travel and discovery by Charles Waterton of nearby **Walton Hall**.

Next we come to the **town hall**, completed in 1880 by T.E. Collcutt, architect of the Savoy Hotel in London. Experts describe the building as 'French Gothic', and it comes complete with a tall tower which stands out on the skyline from any direction. Opposite is the Victorian police station, and next to it the grand 19th-century **Court House**, complete with an Old Bailey-style statue of justice on the roof.

Next comes the **County Hall**, once the meeting place of both the defunct West Riding and the County Council authorities, and now the home of the City of Wakefield Borough Council. Built in the 1890s it has a richly decorated interior. Further on is **St John's Square**, an impressive ensemble of Georgian townhouses whose grandeur serves to emphasise the wealth of Wakefield two centuries ago. Also here is the **church of St John**, built at the end of the 18th century and entirely in keeping with the rest of the square.

Other interesting locations in the city include the first-class indoor and outdoor markets and the **City Art Gallery** on Wentworth Terrace. Most important among the exhibits are early works by Henry Moore, who hailed from nearby Castleford, and Wakefield's own sculptor of international repute, Barbara Hepworth. Lovers of literature, especially the realist school, will enjoy a visit to the **Gissing Centre** on Thompsons Yard off Westgate. This is the birthplace of the gloomy George, whose single-minded determination to show Victorian England and its failings in an accurate light ensured historians a wealth of detail. Gissing's life story is like a novel itself. He was expelled from university for pickpocketing from his fellow students. He needed the money to help a prostitute that he had decided to reform. He caught syphilis from her, but married her nonetheless, and when she died fell for another lady of easy virtue. Sounds more like a soap opera than Victorian middle-class respectability!

No visit to Wakefield would be complete without a close look at the **Chantry Chapel of St Mary** on Wakefield Bridge. Built in the 1340s, this is one of only four such structures still remaining (the others are in nearby Rotherham, at Bradford-on-Avon and St Ives in Cambridgeshire). Said to be by far the best of the quartet, the purpose of the chapel was to serve as a shelter for those wishing to cross the Calder and enter the medieval town. It also collected alms for the upkeep of the bridge. Historians record that as early as 1580 the façade of the building was badly defaced. Restored in the 19th century by Sir George Gilbert Scott, the original now adorns the boathouse at Newmillerdam, a beauty spot on the city's boundary. The façade comes complete with fine reliefs of the Annunciation, Nativity, Resurrection, Ascension and Pentecost. Inside there is a small crypt reached via a spiral staircase. The chapel housed plague victims in the 1500s to prevent their pestilence infecting the citizens across the river, and also served as a shop and a newspaper office. The **bridge** itself is also medieval and has nine pointed arches.

Wakefield has a number of pleasant civic parks of Victorian origin, but much newer is **Pugneys Country Park** off the Denby Dale Road. A man-made water feature, it is busy every weekend with sailing and windsurfing fanatics, while a path and cycle route encircle the water. On the far side of the main lake is a small wildlife reserve, complete with reed-beds and water on which wildfowl overwinter and breed.

WALSDEN [Calderdale]

SD9322: 9 miles (14km) N of Rochdale

This is a typical Pennine town situated in the Calder Gap between Yorkshire and Lancashire. The Rochdale Canal, which runs through the valley, brought jobs and prosperity, but now little home-grown industry survives. Its cricket team is one of the best in the region, and once employed as its only playing professional the great Sir Clive Lloyd, captain of Lancashire and West Indies. He is famed for once hitting a ball so high in the air in a local match at Walsden that it fell to earth some time later covered in snow. Howzat for modern-day folklore?

WALTON [Wakefield]

SE3517: 3 miles (5km) SE of Wakefield

This is a pleasant rural village on the edge of Wakefield, complete with its own traditional community but also popular with those who wish to commute to work. The **Barnsley Canal**, which came right through the village in 1799, can still be seen. It once served the many coal mines which pock-marked this whole area.

The main reason for visiting Walton, though, is to pay homage to the memory of Squire Charles Waterton. If ever there were a great English eccentric, it was this heir to his family's ancient fiefdom at **Walton Hall**. Built in 1767, this classical Georgian pile sits on an island in the middle of a picturesque lake. It replaced a 15th-century manor house, the **watergate** of which – complete with carved stone cross – still survives. The island is linked to the rest of the park by a graceful, 18th-century, cast-iron bridge.

Born there 15 years after the new house was completed, Charles was educated at the great Catholic school at Stonyhurst in North Yorkshire before travelling to Latin America during the Napoleonic Wars. A member of a privileged class at an inquiring time in European history, Waterton embraced science, and particularly natural history, with gusto. Wandering through the Amazon rainforest in bare feet and accompanied by local people, he survived a bout of fever, beat off a boa constrictor with his fists and one hooked and rode a Cayman alligator. Collecting specimens as he went – which he then stuffed and brought home (look in **Wakefield Museum** for some examples) – he wrote books on his travels and there is no doubt he was a scientist of considerable importance.

Back home in Yorkshire, he proceeded to turn his estate into a nature reserve, probably the first in the country. He built a high stone wall around the boundaries to keep out poachers and others who might disturb his observations, planted thousands of trees and shrubs to encourage birds and other wildlife, and even built cleverly disguised hides. He is credited with building the first bird nesting boxes, and he installed pipes in walls to attract certain species. Legend has it that he paid youngsters sixpence every time they brought a hedgehog to be released into the park. Eccentric he might have been, he slept on the floor in his mansion with a block of wood for a pillow, but one wonders whether he wasn't the victim of a bad press. When the local vicar came on his regular visits the Squire would flee the house and hide in the grounds, often for the whole day, until the clergyman tired of waiting and went on his way.

Nowadays, the hall is a country club and a golf course takes up part of the park. Nonetheless, there is a network of footpaths in the area, and the designated **Waterton Trail**, which is well worth exploring. Nearby, and another 'must', is **Anglers Country Park**. The result of deep coal mining followed by opencasting, we now have a series of lakes and ponds. In true Waterton tradition, they are a magnet for birds throughout the year as trees and other plants begin to establish themselves. Part of the attraction here is the **Heronry**, an interactive local history and natural history exhibition of interest to young and old alike.

WENTBRIDGE [Wakefield]

SE4916: 4 miles (6km) SE of Pontefract

This small rural hamlet sits on the route of the Great North Road, and consequently has been a stopping-off point for travellers for many years. This is still an agricultural village, although some grand homes also exist, commanding prices to match. The A1 thunders past not far away, but the sound of the traffic is masked by the thick belt of trees which form a backdrop for the village. It is this ancient highway which gives Wentbridge a place in the folklore of, arguably, England's greatest folk hero. Many claim Robin Hood as a son of Yorkshire. The once enormous Sherwood Forest stretched from what is now left of it in Nottinghamshire to a little south of here at **Barnsdale Bar**. In Roman times, the Great North Road from London, then known Roman Ridge, veered west at the Bar and headed across the Aire valley towards Pontefract and a crossing of the river at Castleford.

By the 12th century, travellers were following a more direct northerly route on their way to Ferrybridge across the drier magnesian limestone beds from which Wentbridge's light-coloured buildings are constructed. There were inns and a hospital – a refuge for travellers – at Wentbridge by the 1300s, and by the 17th century there were four inns, one of them known as a haunt of footpads and other ne'er do wells. The early stories of Robin speak of him operating in the area of Barnsdale, some mentioning Wentbridge by name.

Sitting in a hollow of the River Went is **the church of St John**, a red-roofed building constructed as recently as 1878. Limestone rock-faced and cruciform in shape, the church is small and high with apse and chancel.

WEST BRETTON [Wakefield]

SE2813: 4½ miles (7km) SSW of Wakefield

The pretty commuter village of West Bretton is an idyllic rural retreat of honey-coloured houses and a chocolate box cricket pitch. A substantial **war memorial** sits in the centre.

For most visitors though, the reason for coming here – and it is easily reached from junction 38 of the M1 – is the **Yorkshire Sculpture Park**. Based in the grounds of **Bretton Hall**, this is arguably the best free day out in the county. Although there is a small charge for parking, the visitor then has 80 hectares (200 acres) of beautifully landscaped grounds in which to stroll; and one of the finest collections of sculpture in the country to look at and stroke. Although it attracts 200,000 visitors a year, it is never crowded. The sculptures from a whole range of styles and disciplines are positioned discreetly amongst the trees, or more formally on the grand garden terraces of the former mansion.

The permanent collection is huge and important, including work by Wakefield's own Barbara Hepworth. One of her most important collections of bronzes was stolen a few years ago by thieves who used a crane and truck to carry them away; thankfully they were rescued from a scrap-yard before those responsible could melt them down. Other artists whose work can be seen here include the late, great, Elisabeth Frink, Rodin, Turner Prize-winner Grenville Davey, Gio Pomodoro and David Nash. In addition, there are changing exhibitions to stretch the mind, and occasionally, the credulity, of the visitor.

A particularly attractive area is the walled **Bothy Garden**, which not only has indoor and outdoor exhibition areas – including the lovely Pavilion Gallery – but also a shop and restaurant. There are works to interest the children, and a sculpture trail designed for people with disabilities.

As if this were not enough, beside the park are another 40 hectares (100 acres) designated as **Bretton Country Park**. Here, where sheep and cattle graze while picnickers enjoy their sandwiches, is a permanent exhibition of works by Henry Moore. These huge creations by the Castleford-born artist seem so much at home here, despite their 'modern' appearance, that one can't help marvelling at the creative genius of the man. There are several waymarked walks around the grounds, taking in the **Lower Lake** and its waterfowl via the impressive early 19th-century **Cascade Bridge**.

Nearby, but closed to the public, is the 18th-century **Bretton Chapel**, built as a place of worship for the residents of **Bretton Hall**. This latter building is also closed to the public but is being put to good use as a teacher training centre of high repute. The exterior of the building, created in 1720 for Sir William Wentworth (another of this ubiquitous Yorkshire landowning clan), with its nine bays can be admired. The nearby **Camelia House** is open to visitors. It was constructed, complete with Tuscan columns, in 1817 by Sir Jeffrey Wyatville. It was an ideal home for what were then rare and valuable plants.

WEST HARDWICK [Wakefield]

SE4118: 4½ miles (7km) E of Wakefield

This tiny village not far from Nostell Priory is worth an outing as it is the home of **Top Farm Agricultural Museum**. Despite being in the heart of the West Yorkshire coalfield, this is agricultural country, with huge flat fields stretching away on all sides.

The museum has a good collection of farm implements, tractors, tools and other items from the 19th century. Most of the artefacts were collected locally. In addition, there are animals to feed in a welcoming setting.

WETHERBY [Leeds]

SE4048: 2 miles (3km) N of Boston Spa

Another staging post on the Great North Road, Wetherby has an appearance and ambience more akin to genteel North Yorkshire than the gritty industrialised West Riding. Part of the latter it nonetheless was, and the contrast with its neighbours makes it well worth a day trip – especially on Thursdays when the market is in full swing. Once an agricultural centre for the villages and farms roundabout, it was inevitable a town would grow up here once a safe crossing of the River Wharfe had been established. The current **bridge** is thought to be able to count two of its six arches as early medieval. Downstream is a great weir, also of medieval date and almost certain to have powered at least one mill, which has recently been restored and can be admired from a pleasantly maintained picnic area.

Just outside the town are the limited remains of Wetherby Castle, thought to have been built at the time of the conquest by the Knights Templars.

The prosperity of the town in Georgian times is clear from the many fine buildings that survive, all in a warm, glowing stone. The **church of St James** was constructed at the beginning of the Victorian era with fine lancet windows.

The old bridge, Wetherby

WHITKIRK [Leeds]

SE3634: 4 miles (6km) E of Leeds

This small town is now to all intents and purposes yet another suburb of Leeds. Yet in the Middle Ages it was a settlement worthy of its own **parish church of St Mary** – a building of particular value for lovers of architecture. Apart from a new chancel added in 1901, the church is built almost entirely in the Perpendicular style, probably in the 14th century. A chantry chapel was added in the 15th century, and a collection of **funerary monuments** adds particular interest. Especially moving are those to the Viscount Irwin of Temple Newsome who died in 1688, together with that of his widow (died 1746) and their two-year-old daughter, seen morbidly staring at a skull.

Also here is the resting place of locally born engineer John Smeaton (1724-94); his funerary tablet includes a representation of the third Eddystone Lighthouse. The structure was designed by him in 1756 and operated until 1877, when it was replaced and rebuilt on Plymouth Hoe where it still stands today. Smeaton was also responsible for Ramsgate harbour and no less a feat than the Forth and Clyde Canal.

WIBSEY [Bradford]

SE1430: 2 miles (3km) SW of Bradford

This is an ancient settlement and one which developed in a similar way to many others in the county until the onset of industrialisation at the start of the 19th century. Until then most families would have farmed a piece of common land, raised a few animals and probably worked in their own homes spinning and weaving wool. There is a good selection of 16th- and 17th-century buildings still to be seen. Iron and coal deposits were considerable hereabouts and in the 1900s the township grew to accommodate the new trades.

The town is probably best known for the legendary Wibsey Fair. Reputed to be the oldest horse fair in the country, it is believed to have been founded by the monks of **Kirkstall Abbey** in the 12th century. Traders came from miles around to do business at the autumn fair, when horses would have been run up and down **Folly Hall Road** to demonstrate their value. Particularly distressing must have been the 'ketty fair' on the last day when old nags would be sold off to the knacker's men.

WIKE [Leeds]

SE3242: 2 miles (3km) SE of Harewood

Always a rural hamlet, Wike still boasts no more than a couple of dozen homes, and no electric street lighting. Of special interest is the old **School House**, founded in 1726 by Lady Betty Hastings from **Ledston Hall** near Leeds. During the week the building was used for the education of local children and a cottage for the schoolmistress was attached. At the weekend their desks would be turned around to act as pews for Sunday worship.

WILSHAW [Kirklees]

SE1110: 2 miles (4km) NW of Holmfirth

Until the 19th century, this small village was little more than the odd farm settlement set amongst woods. Then along came Joseph Hirst, a canny chap who successfully exploited the large amounts of home-produced woollen textiles being produced in this part of what is now Kirklees. At a time when new technology, in the form of factory-sized machines, was being introduced, he was among the first to adopt them. His mill, houses for his workers and even a school for their children helped create the Wilshaw of today. He even built St Mary's Church in 1863 and named it in tribute to his wife. He, too, is buried in the churchyard. The mill and its chimney might have gone, but the church with its central tower remains to remind us of a time when men really could make a mark on their communities – for better or worse.

WINTERSETT [Wakefield]

SE3815: 4 miles (6km) SE of Wakefield

There aren't many houses with an address in Wintersett as the place is best known for the reservoir of this name. Nearby, though, is the town of Ryhill, via which visitors would have come by train for a Sunday afternoon stroll. Built in 1854, the reservoir was constructed to serve the nearby Barnsley Canal. Two decades later, and just a short distance away, Cold Hiendley Reservoir was created for the same purpose. These two expanses of water, together with the newer Anglers Lake nearby, constitute an extremely important reserve for breeding and wintering birds.

Cutting of the canal began in 1793 at Heath, near Wakefield. It carried coal from Barnsley and stone and groceries from Wakefield. Nowadays the waterway, which closed in 1954, is so attractive to birds and insects that it has been designated a site of Special Scientific Interest.

WOODKIRK [Leeds]

SE2725: 5 miles (8km) SSE of Leeds

This small village not far from Dewsbury is sometimes known as West Ardsley, but the main building of interest in the settlement has Woodkirk in its title. The church of St Mary is largely dated to the year 1831 when it was rebuilt using money from the Church Commissioner's second 'Waterloo Fund' – money set aside to extend the Church of England's influence at a time of growing interest in Nonconformism. What predates this though, and makes a visit to Woodkirk worthwhile, is the ancient church tower dating from the middle of the 13th century at the latest. It is in the Early English style and has a fine Jacobean pulpit and panelled chancel stalls dating from the 1400s.

WOOLLEY [Wakefield]

SE3213: 5 miles (8km) SSW of Wakefield

Racing along the M1, few would imagine that just a couple of tranquil miles away is one of the most pleasant villages in this part of the county; a rural idyll in which the house prices match the ambience. Up until 30 years ago Woolley had its own colliery, but that has now closed and a huge slag heap it produced has now been removed and the coal left in it restored.

Woolley village, however, is a different place altogether, with many houses – some of them quite grand – dating back to the 18th century. **St Peter's Church** was undoubtedly on the site in Norman times, but what we see today is almost entirely of the 15th century in the Perpendicular style. There is a Norman tympanum – the feature seen above an arch – which has been re-used in the south aisle. Glass in the north and south chapels is dated to the Middle Ages and represents somewhat jumbled figures. The lead used to hold stained glass together rarely survives more than 150 years in serviceable condition, and religious windows throughout Europe have often been re-glazed many times. Perhaps not surprisingly, bits of the window jigsaw are lost, either due to neglect before repairs are carried out or during the work itself. Pevsner speculates that the

The Green, Woolley

pictures we see now are part of much more, hence the less than perfect finished work. Elsewhere in the church, look out for more modern glass dated 1871. These three figures are thought to be the work of Morris & Company, founded by the Arts and Crafts Movement's leader, William Morris.

WRENTHORPE [Wakefield]

SE3122: 2 miles (3km) NW of Wakefield

This is a former largely industrial town with its inevitable coal mining heritage running through its veins. Wrenthorpe didn't get its own church until **St Anne's** was built in 1874. Of note is the stained glass, believed to be the work of the ubiquitous late Victorian designer C.E. Kempe; he was just 37 at the time and his style was still developing.

Until the middle of the 19th century, what we now know as Wrenthorpe was called Potovens due to the large numbers of clay works in the area. From the middle of the 15th century until the end of the 18th the production of clay pipes, vessels and other light products was the mainstay of the community.

Later, the place gained a new name, and a new industry, falling into West Yorkshire's 'Rhubarb Triangle' made up by Leeds, Morley and Wakefield. Cheap coal and coke meant the plant – known locally as 'tusky' – could be forced in darkened sheds in November ready for sale at Christmas.

WYKE [Bradford]

SE1526: 4 miles (6km) SSW of Bradford

This community is now considered part of the city of Bradford, but still retains its own identity and character. Like the village of Fulneck near Pudsey, Wyke had its own community from the Moravian Church and they built their **chapel** here in 1755. It is a plain, rectangular structure with a minister's house next door. The **church of St Mary** was built in 1847.

Select Bibliography

Betjeman, John, *Guide to English Parish Churches* (Harper Collins, 1958)

Bottomley, Frank, *Yorkshire Churches* (Alan Sutton, 1993)

Dibnah, Fred, *Fred Dibnah's Industrial Age* (BBC Worldwide, 1999)

Hadfield, Charles, *British Canals* (David & Charles, 1974)

Humphrey, Stephen (editor), *Churches and Chapels of Northern England* (Blue Guides, 1991)

Kellett, Arnold, *The Yorkshire Dictionary* (Smith Settle, 1994)

Liversidge, Doug, *The Luddites*, (Watts, 1972)

Lloyd, David W., *The Making of English Towns*, (Gollancz, 1984)

Mee, Arthur, *West Yorkshire* (King's England Press, 1941)

Muir, Richard, *The Yorkshire Countryside: A Landscape History* (Keele, 1997)

Pevsner, Nikolaus, *The Buildings of England:Yorkshire West Riding* (Penguin, 1959)

Roberts, Andy, *Ghosts and Legends of Yorkshire* (Jarrold, 1992)

Smith, Duncan & Trevor, *South & West Yorkshire Curiosities* (Dovecote, 1992)

Speakman, Colin, *Shire County Guide:West Yorkshire* (Shire, 1988)

Various authors, *The South & West Yorkshire Village Book* (Countryside Books/S & W Yorkshire Federations of Women's Institutes, 1991)

Index

Also of interest from:

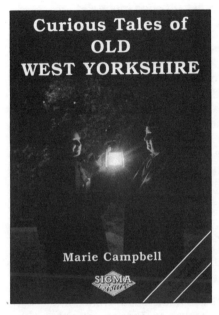

CURIOUS TALES OF OLD WEST YORKSHIRE
Marie Campbell

Written in a gripping, almost gothic style this title is a seriously researched compendium of all things connected with the strange side to West Yorkshire: battles hard-fought upon the bleak moors, ancient folklore, superstition, witchcraft and wizardry of the Old Faith.

"In this fascinating, entertaining, bustling...package of oddities, Marie Campbell ranges far and wide."
BRADFORD TELEGRAPH & ARGUS

£7.95

BEST TEA SHOP WALKS IN WEST YORKSHIRE
Norman & June Buckley

Perfect for family excursions with an in-built reward!

Join Norman and June – Britain's best-known proponents of the twin pleasures of country walks and charming English tea shops. The walks are conveniently based on the major conurbations of West Yorkshire and they are all of a leisurely nature, with a tea shop *en route*, at the end of the walk - or both!

£6.95

WEST YORKSHIRE WALKS: CALDERDALE
Martin Brewis

Calderdale is a popular walking area with a variety of open moorland, valleys and villages to explore.

On these 25 walks, you'll enjoy walking in the dramatic Pennine landscape of Calderdale. Explore its bustling markets and mill shops in the textile manufacturing heartland of England, visit such facinating old towns as Halifax and Hebden Bridge - or see historic stately homes set in peaceful parkland.

£7.95

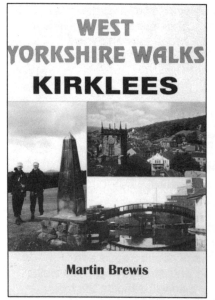

WEST YORKSHIRE WALKS: KIRKLEES
Martin Brewis

Kirklees lies at the south-west corner of West Yorkshire. Though usually associated with the old textile towns of Cleckheaton, Heckmondwike or Wakefield, there are many attractive villages such as Denby Dale and Holmfirth to delight the walker. Once in the countryside, there are high ridges with breathtaking panoramic views, or the valleys of the Holme, Colne and Spen rivers which once powered the area's industries. 25 detailed routes await the discerning walker.

£7.95

All of our books are available through your local bookseller. In case of difficulty, or for a free catalogue, please contact:
SIGMA LEISURE, 1 SOUTH OAK LANE, WILMSLOW, CHESHIRE SK9 6AR.
Phone: 01625-531035; Fax: 01625-536800.
E-mail: sigma.press@zetnet.co.uk . Web site: http//www.sigmapress.co.uk

VISA and MASTERCARD welcome.